RAISING ME

Raising me raises him.
Raising me raises a society.

Hanaa Alabri

Raising Me
Copyright © 2025 Hanaa Alabri
First published in 2025

Print: 978-1-76124-256-4
E-book: 978-1-76124-257-1
Hardback: 978-1-76124-258-8
UAE MEDIA: MC-02-01-3058931
Date: 5th December 2025

All rights reserved. No part of this book may be reproduced, stored in a retrieval system, or transmitted by any means (electronic, mechanical, photo-copying, recording, or otherwise) without written permission from the author.

Because of the dynamic nature of the Internet, any web addresses or links contained in this book may have changed since publication and may no longer be valid. The information in this book is based on the author's experiences and opinions. The views expressed in this book are solely those of the author and do not necessarily reflect the views of the publisher; the publisher hereby disclaims any responsibility for them.

The author of this book does not dispense any form of medical, legal, financial, or technical advice either directly or indirectly. The intent of the author is solely to provide information of a general nature to help you in your quest for personal development and growth. In the event you use any of the information in this book, the author and the publisher assume no responsibility for your actions. If any form of expert assistance is required, the services of a competent professional should be sought.

Publishing information
Publishing and design facilitated by
Passionpreneur Publishing
A division of Passionpreneur Organization Pty Ltd
ABN: 48640637529

Melbourne, VIC | Australia
www.passionpreneurpublishing.com

Contents

Contents	iii
Dedication	v
Testimonials	vi
Acknowledgements	xi
Introduction	1
PREPARING	**9**
Who is the Child?	11
How to Parent?	31
What is a Family?	49
PRACTISING	**67**
Am I Observant?	69
Am I Sensing?	89
Am I Reflecting?	111
PROGRESSING	**141**
Are We Accepting?	143
Are We Advocating?	165
Are We Inclusive?	183

Conclusion	201
Endnotes	205
Author Bio	207
Glossary	209

Dedication

I give this book to my son, Ilyas.
Seeing the world through your eyes is enchanting!

Testimonials

Dr Hilary Cottam, author of *Radical Help*:

"In this brave and beautiful book Hanaa Alabri charts the course of raising her neuro divergent child in Emirati society. Referring to 'the artistry of parenting' she recounts the emotions like desert winds—her own and her son's—with unflinching honesty, as she navigates the every day, reactions of family and friends and encounters with professionals who can help or obstruct. These are the stories we need to guide the design of social systems in which all of us—children, families and wider society—can flourish today."

Marilena di Coste, Founder and CEO, The Butterfly:

"I have had the privilege of knowing Hanaa, the mother of Ilyas, through The Butterfly community. As part of our parents' support group, Hanaa has always stood out as a resilient mother, deeply committed to her son's journey with autism.

This book is a meaningful contribution, not only to share her story, but also to help many other families better understand the challenges and opportunities of living with disability. It highlights the power of advocacy and the importance of building a truly inclusive society.

As the founder of The Butterfly, I am honoured to support Hanaa in this endeavour. I wish her every success with this book, and I wish Ilyas a life filled with dignity, fulfilment, and value that enriches us all. May Hanaa's voice inspire many and open doors to greater inclusion."

Saeed Al Qashbari, Sign Language Interpreter, Zayed Higher Organization (ZHO):

"شكر وتقدير لأم طفل التوحد, نعبر عن امتناننا لجهودكم المضاعفة، وصبركم، ودعمكم المستمر لطفلكم وايضاً لمشروعكم الفريد، وتفانيكم في فهم عالم واحتياجات التوحد. ورسالتكم الملهمة في إصدار كتابكم, وفقكم الله لما فيه منفعة لأصحاب الهمم من التوحد"

اخوكم / سعيد القشبري

مترجم لغة الإشارة / مؤسسه زايد العليا لأصحاب الهمم

Translated: "I would like to express our gratitude and appreciation to the mother of an autistic child for her tireless efforts, patience, and ongoing support for her child and her unique project, as well as her dedication to understanding the world and needs of autism. We also commend her inspiring message in her book, which we hope will benefit those with autism."

Dr. Sharifa Yateem, BCBA:

"As I read through the key insights of this book, my first reaction was "Wow." These pages highlight the true foundational principles of an inclusive system. It is both refreshing and inspiring to see how a mother has transformed her lived experience into a resource that professionals in the neurodiversity field can genuinely benefit from. The book not only provides practical understanding, but it also nurtures empathy and encourages a meaningful shift in perspective—something I believe is essential before stepping into this profession.

As I began reading the first chapter, something immediately resonated with me—it echoed the voices of the mothers I meet every day in my clinic, sharing similar experiences and emotions. As an Emirati Behavior Analyst, I truly hope that current and future mothers will have the opportunity to read your book. It captures the Emirati cultural perspective in a way that many psychologists and behavior analysts may not fully understand—particularly the realities of daily life and how shifts within the family dynamic deeply shape motherhood. Your work brings these truths to light with authenticity, compassion, and strength."

Dr. Roeia Thabet, Educational Specialist:

"I have known Hanaa for many years, as a mother, an intellectual, a professional working mom, and a dear loving friend. Throughout the years, she has consistently demonstrated remarkable perseverance, deep spiritual insight, and a pure heart. Raising Me book is a reflection of these very qualities, a heartfelt journey that beautifully blends strength with kindness, intellect with empathy, and motherhood with sense of purpose. Through her words and actions, Hanaa inspires us to embrace inclusion, compassion, and the transformative power of love that uplifts both ourselves and our communities. Her story is not only inspiring but also a reminder that growth, transformation, and empathy begin at home, within our families, and radiate outward to enrich society as a whole."

Choi Changhoon, Author and Korean Government Official:

"The journeys of Hanaa Alabri and Ilyas illuminate the path toward which the UAE's society progresses. Their moving stories are awaited with heartfelt anticipation. May their families be ever blessed."

Acknowledgements

In the quiet spaces between the words of this book lies the profound influence of so many souls whose paths have intertwined with mine—friends, colleagues, and fleeting encounters that have left indelible marks on my heart. To each of you who listened with open ears to my vulnerabilities, shared in the raw conversations of struggle and triumph, and offered a compassionate presence amid the uncertainties of raising Ilyas, I extend my deepest gratitude. Your kindness has been the unseen thread weaving strength into my journey, reminding me that we are never truly alone in our quests for understanding and inclusion.

A special note of thanks goes to Moustafa Hamwi, whose guidance and belief helped breathe life into this book, transforming my reflections into a shared narrative of hope.

I am grateful to Natasa Denman, whose inspiration ignited my writing spark years ago, encouraging me to capture these stories long before I found the courage to do so.

My heartfelt appreciation flows to Monika Bylinka, the first and only Board Certified Behaviour Analyst (BCBA) who crossed our threshold with a bag brimming with toys, evaluating Ilyas's needs in the warmth of our home without a single charge. In a world often driven by transactions, Monika's humanity shone brightly—she listened, guided, and remained a steadfast companion through our twists and turns, always responsive to our fears and flexible in her approach. Her empathy not only supported Ilyas but affirmed our family's intuition, creating a partnership built on trust and mutual respect.

To Bahij Khouzami, I offer sincere thanks for his interactive online course on Behavioural Analysis, which empowered parents like me to apply practical wisdom at home. His attentiveness to our questions and thoughtful alternatives in the face of our challenges made the learning feel personal and profound.

With boundless love, I honour Lara Kantargian, our devoted Registered Behavioural Therapist, who poured her heart into Ilyas for over fourteen months. Lara became more than a guide—she was family, turning every corner of our home and neighbourhood into a playground of growth, connecting with Ilyas's world and even his schoolmates. Her dedication lingers in our lives, a testament to the power of genuine care.

My warmest regards to Kevin Baskerville, the experienced behaviourist whose friendship and expertise enriched our

ACKNOWLEDGEMENTS

discussions. In sharing my experiences and seeking his insights, I found not just solutions, but a kindred spirit who understood the depths of our path.

Finally, a profound embrace and overflowing gratitude to my dear friend Maryam Mahboubi, whose gentle encouragement drew me into the world of children's classes alongside her. Maryam, with her luminous spirit, has been a steadfast cheerleader for my motherhood, sending heartfelt reviews after each session that celebrated Ilyas's every small victory. Her appreciation for adult progress in teaching children supported the study of the Ruhi Institute's *Book 3: Teaching Children's Classes* with our peers, nurturing souls and fostering the inclusive communities we hold dear.

To all who have walked beside us, your compassion has illuminated the way forward, nourishing the inclusive world this book envisions. Thank you for being the light in our story.

INTRODUCTION

What if the key to raising an inclusive society lies not in changing others, but in first raising ourselves—acknowledging our own flaws, biases, and hidden depths to truly see every soul, from the youngest child to the most seasoned elder, as a noble equal?

Dear reader, whether you are a parent navigating the uncharted waters of neurodivergence, someone dreaming of starting and maintaining a family, or simply a seeker yearning for deeper human connections, I welcome you. This book is for you—the mothers and fathers who feel the weight of isolation in a hurried world, the dreamers who believe we are all children at heart, and those ready to challenge the rigid confines of "normal" to embrace the beauty of diversity.

Imagine discovering that the most transformative story in these pages—the one friends and strangers alike press me about—is not just my son's autism diagnosis, but the raw, humiliating moments that forced me to confront my own limitations as a mother, only to emerge stronger, more empathetic, and determined to fiercely advocate for him. Or consider this startling truth: In our fast-paced era, where digital distractions erode our bonds, neurodivergent individuals like my son Ilyas are not the "problem"—society's insistence on conformity is, often expelling children from schools upon diagnosis, even when they're thriving. Readers like you—parents, educators, and community builders—will be most captivated (and perhaps amazed) by how everyday acts of self-reflection can dismantle these barriers, turning personal struggles into societal shifts. Ask yourself: In a world that pulls us from meaningful ties with our families, neighbours, and friends, how often do you pause to truly see the person before you, beyond labels or expectations?

Envision a life where your interactions bloom with profound depth: Conflicts resolve through empathy, your child's unique light shines undimmed, and your community transforms into a haven of belonging. This book offers you a roadmap to reclaim those connections, fostering happy families and open societies where neurodivergence is celebrated as a gift, not a burden—leaving you empowered, inspired, and ready to weave inclusion into every thread of your world.

Through these pages, you'll uncover several key insights:

1. How self-awareness as a parent unlocks deeper bonds with your child, turning challenges like autism into opportunities for growth.

2. How to develop practical traits—observing, sensing, and reflecting—to empathise with neurodivergent sensitivities and build resilient relationships.
3. The myth of "normal", and how redefining it creates inclusive ecosystems that honour diverse abilities.
4. Advocacy strategies to navigate systemic barriers, from therapies to schools, ensuring every individual thrives.
5. The ripple effect of family values on society, inspiring you to extend compassion beyond your home.

As an Emirati mother raising Ilyas, my autistic son, I've walked this path firsthand—navigating diagnoses, therapies, and societal judgements while drawing on my cultural roots, behavioural analysis training, and reflections as a working professional. My journey, enriched by spiritual practices and community advocacy, has equipped me to share these truths with authenticity and heart.

This book serves you by reigniting those lost connections, empowering you to see yourself and others with fresh eyes so you can nurture happier families, kinder communities, and a world where everyone reaches their potential. It's about personal growth: the joy of authentic bonds, the relief of breaking free from perfectionism, and the fulfilment of contributing to an inclusive legacy.

This is a heartfelt guide to personal and societal transformation through parenting and empathy; it is *not* a clinical manual on autism treatments, nor a prescriptive blueprint for "perfect" family life, but an invitation to embrace imperfection and diversity in all its forms.

As we embark on this journey, let's begin by unravelling the essence of the child—who they truly are, beyond labels—and how that revelation reshapes us all. Turn the page to discover the profound question that ignited my path: Who is the child?

Timeline

# on chart	Year	Description	Centre as named in the book
1	2020 Jan	Ilyas is born	
2	2021 Mar	Ilyas tries his first nursery for one week	Nursery #1
3	2021 Sep - Nov	Started speech therapy (ST)	Clinic #1
4	2021 Dec– 2022 Dec	Moved to another clinic for ST and occupational therapy (OT); later in the year behavioural therapy (ABA) was added to Ilyas's intervention schedule. *	Clinic #2
5	2022 Jan–Apr	Ilyas starts at the Montessori nursery	Nursery #2
6	2022 Jan	Visited a clinic associated with stem cells (SC) to explore other solutions for autism	Clinic #3
*7	2022 Mar–Apr	First ABA sessions at Clinic #2 for two weeks	Clinic #2
8a	2022 July–Dec	Started summer camp at a new nursery in our new neighbourhood	Nursery #3
8b	2023 Jan–Aug	Ilyas continued at Nursery #3 for a full academic year and engaged in all seasonal camps.	Nursery #3

INTRODUCTION

# on chart	Year	Description	Centre as named in the book
9	2022 Aug	Ilyas's doctor suggested doing the autism assessment	Clinic #2
10	2022 Nov–Dec	Appointment with a new doctor for the autism assessment that was concluded after 4 evaluation sessions	Hospital #1
11	2022 Jan–Feb	Explored ST and OT sessions at a public clinic and two private clinics	Clinic #4, 5, 6
12	2023 Jan–2024 Feb	Started intensive home ABA therapy with a therapist from Clinic #2	Clinic #2
13a	2023 July	Recruited a Learning Support Assistant, also known as Shadow Teacher.	LSA #1
13b	2024 Feb	First LSA falters in her performance at School#1, hence replacing her.	LSA #1
14	2023 Sep–Dec	Started new academic year at a new nursery	Nursery #4
15	2023 Oct	Board Certified Behaviour Therapist attended Nursery #4 to coach LSA#1 and coordinate with school's Inclusion Manager.	Clinic #2 and Nursery #4
16a	2024 Jan–Jul	Ilyas started Term 2 of foundation stage 1 (FS1) at school	School #1
16b	2025 Jan–Jul	Ilyas continues his education.	School #1
17	2024 Feb–present	New shadow teacher started working with Ilyas at his school on a 12-month contract	LSA #2
18	2024 Mar–Apr	Tried home ABA therapy with a new clinic for 5 weeks	Clinic #7
19	2024 Apr	Explored another clinic for behavioural therapy but only attended one week of assessments at the clinic	Clinic #8
20	2024 May	Saw doctor for evaluating Ilyas to get approval for school therapy	Hospital #2

# on chart	Year	Description	Centre as named in the book
21a	2024 June	Started school therapy of ST and OT provided by clinic under Hospital #2 network.	Clinic #9
21b	2024 August	School therapy continued in the clinic during summer break and then picked up again at school with start of new academic year in September 2024.	Clinic #9
22	2024 Jul	Intensive 2 weeks of mixed therapies in Dubai during summer break	Clinic #10
22	2024 Aug–Sep	Continued therapy in the weekends	Clinic #10
23	2024 Dec	Winter break from school took the opportunity to start swimming classes	Sports #1
24	2025 Nov	Evaluation done at government hospital to apply for People of Determination (POD) card	Hospital #4
25	2024 Dec, 13 and 17	Started exploring SC. Visited a doctor who collaborated in writing research about SC, who referred to another doctor for his expertise in the field of paediatric psychology to explore SC treatment	Clinic #3 and Clinic #11
26	2025 Feb, 13	Second opinion sought for reliable occupational therapy	Clinic #12
27	2025 end of Mar	Stem cell treatment in Serbia	Clinic #13
28	2025 April	Consult for Hyperbaric Oxygen Therapy	Hospital #3
29	2025 July	Intensive behavioural and speech therapies at summer camp in a specialised centre	Nursery #5
30	2025 Sep	Started the new academic year with his classmates at the same school	School #1

INTRODUCTION

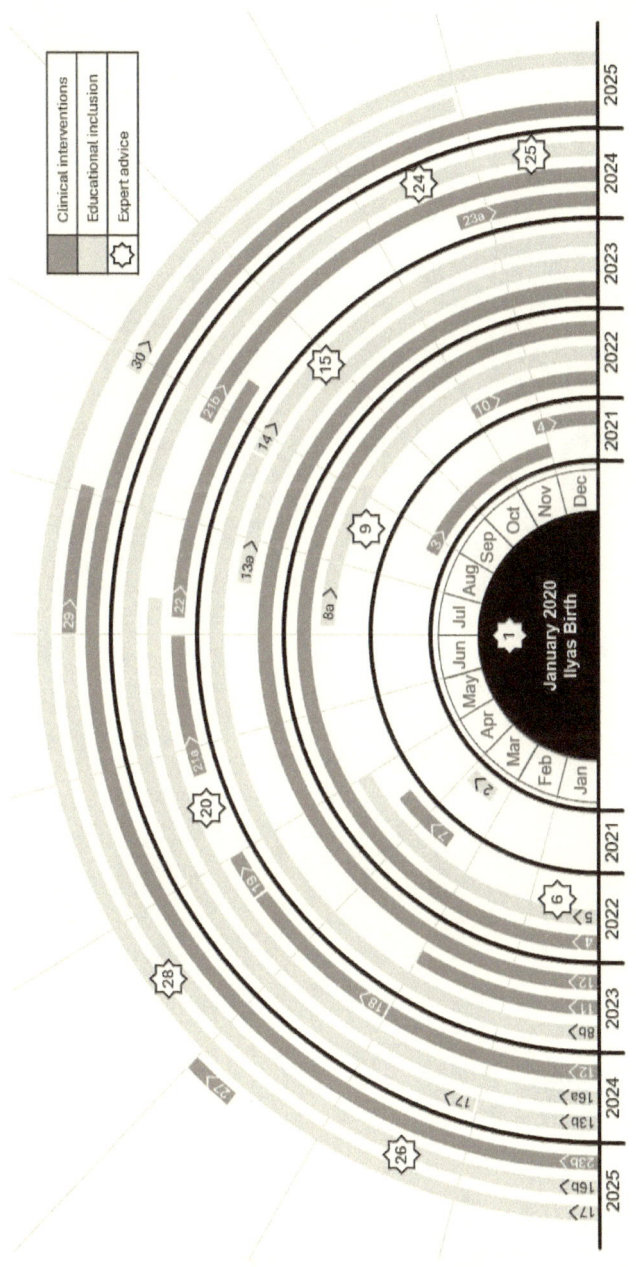

SECTION 1

PREPARING

In this opening section, I explore the essential figures that converge to mould a human being, from the innocence of childhood to the profound act of ushering new life into existence. Throughout the chapters "Who Is the Child?", "How to Parent", and "What Is a Family?", I interweave fragments of my own narrative as an Emirati mother raising Ilyas, my autistic son, illuminating the lessons gleaned and insights forged in the crucible of our shared journey.

Existence in our contemporary world is a tapestry riddled with diversions, ones that mere prayer and spiritual rituals cannot wholly dispel. The arrival of a child, however, acts as a rupture, compelling us to pause, reevaluate, and regain our bearings amid the spiritual and material realms.

These initial chapters illuminate the core elements of a family: the children who embody potential and the parents who nurture it. Each element assumes a pivotal role in constructing this basic unit of society, much like bricks meticulously layered to erect the sturdy walls of a home. Families, in turn, form the indissoluble foundation upon which civilisations rise.

As we unearth the vital responsibilities of family members, we reveal how truly inclusive societies are rooted in deep family bonds. Along the way, we'll embrace neurodivergence not as an aberration, but as a vital thread in our human fabric.

1

WHO IS THE CHILD?

We are all children at heart

For the first 18 months of my son's life, I simply called him "the baby" or "the child". Saddled with multiple unknowns, I was a distant mother with undiagnosed post-partum in the midst of a pandemic, trying to nurture an autistic baby who couldn't even cry to communicate his need for milk.

This chapter delves into the profound question of a child's identity, weaving a tapestry of my journey as an Emirati mother raising Ilyas, a child with autism, amidst familial discord and cultural expectations. Through personal narratives drawn from my own family struggles, I explore how a child's sense of self blossoms from the delicate interplay between family dynamics, cultural heritage, and innate spirit. By the end of this chapter, you will understand the child as both a unique soul and a mirror of the family's heart, laying the cornerstone for an inclusive society that celebrates diverse abilities over conformity.

A Tapestry of Choice: Deciding to Welcome Ilyas

Two years into our marriage, as the desert sun cast long shadows over our Abu Dhabi home, my husband and I embarked on a delicate conversation about welcoming a child. His steady yet probing voice raised thoughtful concerns: the time and resources needed to nurture a young soul, the patience to guide a fledgling spirit through life's earliest stages, the duty to impart worldly wisdom, and the love to cultivate spiritual depth. I listened, my fingers tracing the edge of my mug, but my heart danced elsewhere, brushing aside these weighty questions with the breezy confidence of youth. "Can you envision our life without a child?" I countered, my words light but resolute. If a child was our destiny, why delay the journey? In my naivety, I saw motherhood as a natural unfolding, like a date palm blossoming in season.

My impulsive argument prevailed, and we planned for Ilyas's arrival, aiming for the poetic date of February 2, 2020. Yet, like a desert breeze shifting unexpectedly, he arrived two weeks early, a reminder of life's untamed rhythm. My pregnancy was smooth, buoyed by cursory readings on parenthood and my mother's eager promises to embrace her first grandchild. Her enthusiasm painted a picture of shared burdens, lightening my expectations. But my family's support waned as Ilyas entered our world, their lives entangled in their own unresolved conflicts, as I had witnessed in my own childhood. Grown in years but not in wisdom, my parents remained tethered to material concerns, their voices sharp with discord, their absence a heavy weight on my heart. I had hoped Ilyas, the first of a new generation, would be their priority, a beacon uniting us. Their distance left me to navigate motherhood alone instead, sustained only by my husband's steadfast presence.

Five years later, with the wisdom of hindsight, I see the cost of our delay. Youth brims with energy to chase a child's boundless spirit, sharing in their joys (building sandcastles, splashing in the pool) rather than tethering them to adult constraints (sitting still while I finish work, behaving to avoid strangers' stares, or curbing their movements to protect fragile objects).

Yet I cherish weaving Ilyas into the fabric of daily life. At the market, he learns the rhythm of mundane chores amid the vibrant hues of spices and the scent of fresh bread, even if I only secure a few items from my grocery list. Each trip builds his patience, his small hands reaching for a familiar fruit. Ilyas watches when my husband inflates our Intex pool, absorbing the process until one day he fetches the hose himself, his steps assured as if anticipating the next task. I once brought him to an hour-long hair treatment at a salon overlooking the shimmering Emirates Palace, with the sea's gentle waves a soothing backdrop. Armed with activities to keep him engaged, I ensured his curiosity didn't disrupt the salon's delicate balance of inclusion and care.

Shadows of Care: A Family's Dance Around a Newborn

Six months into my pregnancy, as the desert winds whispered of new beginnings, my husband faced the sudden loss of his job—a challenge softened by the profound gift of impending fatherhood. What first appeared as hardship soon revealed itself as a hidden blessing, giving him a full year to hold our newborn close during his earliest days. My husband stepped into his role with quiet dedication, timing feedings with gentle precision, lulling Ilyas to sleep with soothing rhythms, and perfectly warming every bath. His attentive ear caught the subtle shades of Ilyas's cries—whether signalling hunger, weariness, or the twinge of colic—interpreting them with the care of a devoted guardian. In our Emirati tradition, new mothers often return to their family home for Nafas, those sacred forty days of rest surrounded by loved ones. Yet I chose the intimacy of our own space, grounded by my husband's unwavering support. Even so, my relatives and friends couldn't picture a new mother getting proper care in such a modest space without extra help. After hearing their concerns over and over, I finally agreed to try Nafas at my parents' house. It lasted only two days, as the demands of childcare fell largely

WHO IS THE CHILD?

to me amid their own daily rhythms—my mother tending to meals with her familiar clatter of pots, my father handling errands, and my brother immersed in his pursuits. This experience strengthened my decision to nurture our little family on our own terms, like a resilient date palm drawing strength from deep roots in shifting sands.

The joy of Ilyas's arrival unfolded against the backdrop of my parents' personal challenges. Tested by life's complexities and cultural expectations, their long marriage navigated waves of tension—including my father's decision to take a second wife. Revealing deep-seated concerns, their exchanges highlighted the human vulnerabilities we all carry, even as we yearn for harmony.

Grappling with uncertainties while being driven by her protective instincts, my mother sought resolution through heartfelt efforts like filing for Khulu' (divorce) three times, each step a testament to her strength amid emotional tides. These failed cycles of divorce procedures led her to make the bold move of leasing an apartment, setting up a new space, and encouraging my brother and me to gather our belongings from our childhood home. Even though I felt very little pull toward these forgotten items, the process felt like a gentle clearing. As our family driver, Santoosh, fitted curtains on her moving day, my mother stopped by briefly. Ilyas clung to me as he battled a stomach bug, his small frame trembling as I held him. When illness struck again, incapacitating us both, her quick departure to tend to her curtains illuminated the pull of her own priorities in that season of change. Driving to the hospital alone amid his discomfort, getting my son admitted for round-the-clock care with fluid drips, and spending the night away from home, I gained two pieces of wisdom. First, always keep spare clothes for your child and yourself! Secondly, my mother's brief though limited presence underscored the distances life can create, even among those we love.

My father also paid intermittent visits, as competing family dynamics urged choices between loyalties. Whenever I managed to connect with him, my mother's criticism prompted my gentle reply: "A challenging marriage doesn't diminish a father's heart." One Saturday morning, my father arrived at our home with his five-year-old stepson, their laughter echoing from a morning spent exploring Musaffah's (industrial area in Abu Dhabi) tool sheds, weaving through the bustling market, and stopping at a bakery, their hands full of warm, crinkly bags. The boy's bright eyes and bouncy steps sparked a quiet ache in my heart, stirring memories of my own childhood outings with my father—racing through dusty streets, his strong hand guiding me, the world alive with possibility. Those moments, so vivid and fleeting, awoke a jealous child within me. I longed to be that carefree girl again, chasing adventure by his side, and I yearned for Ilyas, my four-year-old son, to know that same joy with his grandfather. This envy wasn't bitter but tender, a reminder that a child's heart still beats within us all, craving connection and wonder. My father's visits were rare, shadowed by family tensions and my mother's sharp words urging me to pick sides in their fractured marriage. Yet, watching him with his stepson, I saw his fatherly love undimmed, and I realised this childlike yearning could guide me as a mother. By embracing that playful, open spirit, rooted in love and curiosity, I could meet Ilyas where he is, turning our daily routines into shared adventures.

As I entered motherhood, my heart brimmed with hope and quiet uncertainty, interlaced with the exhilaration of welcoming Ilyas and the reality of each family member facing their own journeys. Instead of guiding and nurturing my son, my parents were immersed in personal conflicts. Rather than the full embrace I hoped for, their challenges compelled me to shoulder more of the burden, weaving my own path while cradling my son. Amid this dynamic, where grown-ups echoed the vulnerabilities of youth, I pondered: Who is the child?

My precious newborn Ilyas entered a world of strong personalities, each absorbed in their trials, yet his arrival invited us to rediscover our unity. My husband remained a steady light, his calm a gentle counterpoint to the ebb and flow around us. Feeling Ilyas's delicate warmth, I wrestled with the blur of roles: What does motherhood hold when boundaries shift? Those who were meant to anchor me were busily charting their own courses, redefining what it means to parent and grandparent. This enduring question—Who is the child?—pulsed at my core amid the beauty of new life, inspiring me to reimagine family, duty, and love.

A Tempest of Beginnings: Welcoming Ilyas

After thirty-six hours of labour, each moment a gruelling dance of endurance, my son, Ilyas, entered the world not with a gentle cry but with a piercing scream that echoed through the sterile walls of Corniche Hospital. The sound, raw and unyielding, stirred a primal fear within me, my heart racing as I gazed upon his tiny, flushed face. What had I brought into being, and who was this fierce soul? The question lingered, heavy as the antiseptic air. The first days unfurled in a haze of struggle; Ilyas, touched by jaundice, required an extended stay, his fragile body bathed in soft healing light. Each *beep* of the hospital monitors marked time, stretching our separation from the sanctuary of home. Yet, when we finally crossed the threshold of our Abu Dhabi haven after a week, the warmth of my husband's embrace and Ilyas's delicate weight in my arms wove a joy unparalleled, like the first rain nourishing a parched desert. In that sacred space, surrounded by our small family, I began to ponder anew: *Who is the child?* Was it Ilyas, this radiant spark, or was it me, reborn through the trials of motherhood, seeking to understand his light?

In January 2020, as the world trembled under the shadow of a nascent pandemic, I welcomed my son, Ilyas, into a life both radiant and uncertain. From my hospital bed, surrounded by the sterile hum of machines and the sharp scent of antiseptic, I heard whispers of a distant crisis in China, what I now know as COVID-19, but my heart was tethered to the fragile warmth of my newborn in my arms. Visitors spoke of tragedy, their voices tinged with concern—yet I turned inward, consumed by the sacred duty of motherhood. My fastidious nature found solace in the pandemic's call for distance, a shield to protect Ilyas from eager hands, allowing only the closest family to draw near in those tender early months.

Lockdowns wove a cocoon around us as COVID's grip tightened, limiting visits to my family—once weekly, then fortnightly, and eventually to mere phone calls when sniffles arose. A six-week postpartum hospital visit, meant to tend to my wellbeing, left me hollow; the doctor's focus on future family planning dismissed the quiet tremors of my spirit. Looking back, I see now the veiled shadow of mild depression, masked by the whirlwind of caring for a newborn, returning to work remotely, and searching for a nanny to share the load. In those days, I referred to Ilyas as "the child", a formal distance in my words, devoid of the warmth I felt but could not express. Even as I held him close, my fingers tracing his soft skin, my mind churned with worry; I was struggling to discern what was best for us while wading through a deluge of advice from the internet, seasoned mothers, and family traditions.

It was not until June 2021, when I returned to the office after seventeen months of working from home, that a spark of realisation flickered in me. A senior executive casually mentioned the CEO by a nickname, "JoJo". When I expressed surprise, he responded, "Don't you use nicknames?" I admitted, with a pang of realisation, that I had never given Ilyas one, addressing him only as "Ilyas" or at times "the child". He smiled and shared, "In Lebanon, we call Ilyas 'Lalloosa'." Returning home with a lighter heart that evening, I gazed into Ilyas's bright eyes. "Lalloosa," I whispered, the word rolling off my tongue like a soft and playful melody. The shift was profound. Where once I had been reserved, almost mechanical, this nickname wove a thread of tenderness into our bond, softening my motherhood into something vibrant and melodic, like the call of a desert bird at dawn. In that moment, I began to answer the question that lingered: *Who is the child?* Ilyas was not just "the child" but *my* Lalloosa, a unique soul deserving of love and presence, even amidst the chaos of a fractured family and a world in turmoil.

Shifting Views

Society often perceives children, particularly those with neurodivergent conditions like autism, as blank canvases to be shaped into rigid norms or as burdens defined by their deficits. This reductive view strips them of individuality, prioritising "normalcy" over uniqueness. In my early motherhood, I distanced myself from Ilyas by calling him "the child," reflecting a broader societal tendency to fear neurodivergent children's difference rather than embracing their essence. Forcing all children into a standardised mould hinders inclusive growth, ignoring the vibrant diversity of their spirits.

WHO IS THE CHILD?

A child is a singular spark, their identity a delicate weave of familial love, cultural values, and innate temperament. For Ilyas, autism is not a flaw; it's part of his unique rhythm, one I struggled to harmonise with in my early days as a distant, dry mother. But when I called him "Lalloosa", my heart softened. I saw him for who he truly is: a whole, radiant human. Families must nurture this individuality, treating children as noble equals rather than projects to mould. This shift redefines inclusion as a celebration of each child's light, fostering societies where differences are not deficits but strengths enriching the collective tapestry.

Research underscores the family's pivotal role in shaping identity. A 2015 study in *Clinical Child and Family Psychology* found that positive parental reinforcement boosts self-esteem in neurodivergent children, enhancing social integration.[i] In Emirati culture, three-generational households traditionally foster curiosity through communal living, yet modern shifts toward nuclear families risk isolating children like Ilyas, whose autism demands intentional connection. My parents' entanglement in their fractured marriage highlighted the cost of neglecting a child's identity, as I yearned for their support to nurture Ilyas's spirit. Conversely, my husband's meticulous decoding of Ilyas's needs exemplified how love shapes a child's sense of self.

The Child's Identity

A child's sense of self—their understanding of who they are as an individual—begins to take shape within the family, the first and most intimate environment they encounter. The family acts as a mirror, reflecting the child's internalised values, beliefs, and behaviours while providing space for them to express their innate personality. This interplay between external influences and internal traits forms the foundation of the child's identity, influencing how they view themselves and their place in the world.

Family as the Primary Social Framework

As the child's initial social world, the family is where they first learn about relationships, roles, and expectations. Through daily interactions, children absorb cues about their worth, capabilities, and individuality. For example, a child praised for their creativity may come to see themselves as imaginative, while one frequently criticised may internalise feelings of inadequacy. Parents and caregivers are pivotal here, their words, actions, and emotional responses shaping the child's self-perception. A nurturing environment that encourages exploration fosters confidence, whereas a restrictive or overly critical one may stifle self-expression.

Cultural and Familial Values

The family's cultural background and values significantly influence a child's identity. Traditions, religious beliefs, and cultural norms help the child understand what is valued or expected. For instance, a child in a family prioritising academic achievement may develop a strong sense of self tied to intellectual success. By contrast, a family emphasising community involvement might instil a sense of duty or collective identity. These values become part of the child's internal narrative, shaping how they define their own strengths, responsibilities, and aspirations.

The Role of Siblings and Extended Family

Siblings and extended family members also contribute to identity formation. Siblings often serve as both mirrors and contrasts, helping children define themselves through comparison or rivalry. A younger sibling might strive to differentiate themselves from an older sibling's achievements, carving out a unique identity as "the artistic one" or "the funny one". Grandparents, aunts, or uncles may introduce alternative perspectives or stories that enrich a child's understanding of their heritage and place within the family lineage, further anchoring their sense of self.

Individuality Within the Family Unit

The child's innate personality pushes back against the family's attempts to shape them, creating a dynamic interplay. A naturally curious child might challenge family norms and seek to explore beyond established boundaries, while a more reserved child might find comfort in aligning with family expectations. This negotiation between individuality and family influence is critical. For example, a child in a highly structured family might discover their sense of self through small acts of rebellion (like choosing a hobby that differs from parental expectations), while still carrying the family's core values.

External Influences and the Family's Role

As children grow, external influences like peers, school, and media begin to compete with the family's role in shaping identity. However, the family remains a critical filter, helping the child interpret and integrate these outside perspectives. A supportive family can help a child critically assess societal pressures—such as idealised body images or ruthless academic competition—while reinforcing their intrinsic worth. Conversely, a family struggling to provide emotional security may leave a child craving external validation, potentially skewing their self-concept.

Challenges to Identity Formation

Not all family environments foster a positive sense of self. In families marked by conflict, neglect, or dysfunction, a child's identity may be shaped by insecurity or the need to adapt to instability. For instance, a child in a high-conflict household might develop a self-image as a peacemaker, taking on responsibilities beyond their years. These challenges highlight the family's profound impact, as negative dynamics leave lasting imprints on how a child perceives themselves.

The family, then, is the crucible where a child's sense of self is forged. Through love, guidance, conflict, and shared experiences, it provides the raw materials—values, accepted roles, and emotional feedback—that the child uses to construct their identity. This process is not static but evolves as the child grows, carrying the family's influence into their broader interactions with the world.

Why Opt Out of Parenthood, and What Does It Cost Our Shared Future?

As an Arab mother whose heart beats in rhythm with faith and family, I believe one of the sacred union of marriage's deepest callings is to procreate: that is, to pass on our hard-won wisdom, nurture souls who will carry forward the remembrance of Allah (dhikr), and safeguard the continuity of our lineage. Through our children, we weave the next threads of humanity's grand tapestry, raising generations who will inherit our stories, our struggles, and our hopes. As a mother to my precious Ilyas, whose autistic world has taught me the profound beauty in every unique soul, I cannot envision a world diminished by fewer children—a quieter, less vibrant existence where laughter fades and curiosity dims.

Children are the eternal heartbeat of our homes across the UAE and the Gulf, thriving in the warmth of three-generational households where life's cycles unfold in joyous harmony. Parents give birth to children, who in turn marry and bring new life, transforming elders into doting grandparents. In our traditions, sons welcome their brides into the family fold, while daughters weave themselves into their husbands' clans, creating homes brimming with the merry chaos of multiple generations. Grandparents often live long enough to cradle their great-grandchildren, witnessing the dawn of a fourth wave before passing the torch. These bustling abodes, alive with little ones' giggles, endless questions, and pure innocent light, are more than shelters—they are beacons of hope. Today's wide-eyed explorers become tomorrow's innovators; the artists sketching dreams in the sand grow into visionary creators; the brave hearts scaling playground heights evolve into healers saving lives; and the gentle spirits sharing toys blossom into compassionate community pillars. Without this intergenerational symphony, who will sustain the inclusive society we yearn for, one that embraces disabilities visible and hidden—like autism—with open arms?

Yet, I find myself pondering a troubling shift: why are so many in our modern world choosing to forgo this legacy, opting out of parenthood altogether? Is it the fear of an overpopulated planet straining under humanity's weight? The relentless pace of life that leaves no room for nurturing young souls? The drive to secure financial stability before daring to expand one's heart? Or perhaps the harshness of our world—riddled with uncertainties, conflicts, and inequalities—that makes creating new life feel like an act of cruelty? Some confess a lack of confidence, doubting their ability to steward another being through life's storms, while others carry scars from their own mis-parented childhoods, suppressing emotions that whisper, "I cannot risk repeating the pain." These reasons, heartfelt as they may be, paint children not as blessings but as burdens, obstacles to personal freedom or ambition. In my soul, I cannot reconcile this view; my Ilyas, with his profound gaze and unspoken wisdom, is no hindrance—he is my purpose, my enduring legacy, a gift to the Ummah and the future beyond my sight.

Economies falter under the weight of imbalance, communities lose their vibrancy, and the very fabric of inclusion unravels—for who will advocate for the neurodivergent, the disabled, if the next generation shrinks? As Kahlil Gibran so poetically reminds us: "Your children are not your children. They are the sons and daughters of Life's longing for itself. And though they are with you yet they belong not to you. For they have their own thoughts. For their souls dwell in the house of tomorrow, which you cannot visit, not even in your dreams." In this light, each child is a seed sown for a harvest we may never reap, nurtured by mothers and fathers alike, destined to strengthen our nation and build bridges of empathy. As I hold Ilyas close, feeling the rhythm of his breath against mine, I urge us all: let us question these choices not with judgement, but with gentle inquiry, for in embracing parenthood, we honour life's longing and forge a more compassionate, inclusive world in which every soul—neurodivergent or otherwise—can flourish.

As we navigate the profound journey of adulthood, society often impresses upon us the weighty responsibility of bringing new life into the world—a duty that can feel as vast and daunting as the desert horizons of my homeland. Yet, in my heart as a mother of an autistic boy, whose world has taught me to cherish every nuance of human connection, I choose to reframe this narrative. What if we embraced the inner child lingering within each of us, allowing it to guide our parenting with playfulness, innocence, and boundless creativity, rather than rigid constraints? Children, after all, demand attention, but their true essentials remain elegantly simple: unwavering love and steadfast security. Love manifests as tender care, profound respect, shared knowledge, and unyielding consistency; meanwhile, security provides sanctuary, calming and informing the young mind so it can venture forth to explore the wonders of existence.

Beyond these foundations, children infuse families with a vibrant energy that deepens bonds among relatives, revitalising our shared heritage in subtle and profound ways. They serve as living bridges, reinforcing cultural and religious traditions through fresh retellings and rituals, while in mixed marriages (marriage between two coming from different countries/cultures) like my own, they weave together diverse tapestries, fostering harmony amid difference. In this way, they not only illuminate our homes but also model the inclusive society we must build, one where neurodivergent individuals like my son are celebrated for their unique perspectives, not sidelined by misunderstanding. This natural evolution of family life leads us seamlessly to the next chapter: the pivotal role of parents in guiding these young souls toward reaching their fullest potential.

2

HOW TO PARENT?

Nothing and nobody will prepare you for parenthood

"Overactivity on the part of the adult is a risk factor," Loris Malaguzzi cautioned.

In my fervour to nurture Ilyas, I risked eclipsing his autonomy. In the process, I learned that parenting is not a quest for control, but a sacred art of fostering a child's essence through instinct, adaptation, and love.

As we navigate the components of a family, this chapter will dwell on the critical role of parents in identifying themselves, defining their values, and developing the confidence to follow their instincts. While a mother's instinct is spot on more often than not, she must gain the confidence to lead with her instincts. The mother and father might not align on their parenting styles, yet they must align on their values. Each style—paternal and maternal love—will serve its purpose in different stages of their children's upbringing.

Parenting Misconceptions

Society often assumes parenting is an innate skill requiring no practice, or that clinical expertise inevitably surpasses parental wisdom. Yet this misconception marginalises the organic knowledge of mothers and fathers, particularly when raising neurodivergent children. I initially deferred to therapists for Ilyas's autism, only to find their sensory-focused solutions—mini-toilets, behavioural mandates, etc.—missed his true needs, reflecting a broader societal reliance on experts who prioritise checklists over intuition. Unfortunately, the prevalent belief that parents must conform to a universal blueprint dismisses the diversity of family dynamics and the complexity of cultural contexts.

Parenting is a dynamic tapestry woven from instinct, trial, and cultural wisdom. In this shared endeavour, mothers and fathers bring distinct strengths—unconditional maternal love, paternal discipline—that harmonise through the couple's shared values. For neurodivergent children like Ilyas, parenting demands sensitivity to tone and autonomy, treating them as equals rather than subordinates. This process of building inclusive families and societies fosters connection over control. Honed over many generations, parental intuition often surpasses clinical mandates, empowering families to nurture their child's unique light.

A 2022 *International Journal of Management Entrepreneurship* study found that mothers excel in team management[ii] due to nurturing skills honed during parenting, highlighting the overlap between raising children and leading teams. A 2022 *Journal of Social Behavioural and Health Sciences* study noted that parent-led interventions improve outcomes in autistic children[iii] when tailored to individual needs. My childhood values—Islam's call to love others, my father's wisdom to see good in all, my mother's perfectionist standards—shaped my approach. Yet, therapists' insistence on sensory fixes for Ilyas's potty training ignored my intuition (echoing maternal wisdom passed through generations) that he had outgrown mini-toilets, an insight validated by a psychologist who emphasised diet's role in autism management.

Cultivating a Child's Essence: A Triad of Nourishment

Parenting is the sacred art of nurturing a child's growth, essential not only for their flourishing but for the elevation of society as a whole. To raise a child is to tend to their body, mind, and soul, each requiring its own sustenance to thrive. The body is nourished through wholesome sustenance, filling the heart with comfort like the warmth of a shared meal at an iftar table. The mind finds nourishment in the sanctuary of safety and stability provided by a home where soft lights and gentle voices create a haven from life's storms. The soul, radiant and eternal, is cultivated through spiritual enlightenment, deeply rooted in our Islamic faith. As an Emirati mother, I weave spiritual nourishment into daily life—through the rhythmic cadence of salah, the service of zakat, and the worship of Allah, the essence that anchors our souls like a nakhla in the desert. By tending to these three dimensions, we shape children who are whole, resilient, and ready to contribute to a compassionate world, their spirits illuminated by divine light.

A Mother's Faith: Weaving Spirituality Amidst New Truths

In the quiet of our Abu Dhabi home, where the call to prayer drifted through open windows, my family saw me not as a beacon of faith but as a soul adrift, more spiritual than devout. As I cradled my newborn, Ilyas, his soft breaths warm against my skin, their urgent whispers implored me to instil in him the sacred tenets of Islam—the rhythm of salah, the generosity of zakat, the sanctity of worship. Their furrowed brows betrayed their fear: that I, in my perceived lack of religiosity, might fail to pass on Allah's divine teachings, risking the weight of sin upon my soul. Their words, heavy with expectation, stirred a quiet unease within me, yet my heart, rooted in faith, sought to nurture Ilyas's spirit in my own way, like a ghaf tree offering shade to a weary traveller.

When the revelation came that Ilyas lives with Autism Spectrum Disorder (ASD), a truth unveiled through his sensitive reactions to the world (e.g. discomfort with loud family gatherings and textured clothing), I paused to reflect on my duty. I wondered if Allah, in His infinite mercy, had lightened this obligation, as Islamic teachings ease for those with unique challenges. In that moment, gazing into Ilyas's bright, searching eyes, I felt a deeper call—to weave faith into his life not through rigid mandates but through love and understanding, a tapestry of rahma that honoured both his soul and his singular journey.

Parenting is a job, a skill that actually requires training. It involves far more than listening to advice. Nevertheless, no one learns how to parent. We believe it's a given—after all, we were all parented, and will do the same for our children. I did not think parenting needs practice, but reflecting on my childhood during my pregnancy, I identified the values that stuck with me no matter what. I then divided them into their source, singling out what resonated the most from my three sources of values:

- From religion (Islam):
  - Love for others what you love for yourself
  - Verily some suspicion is sinful.

- From my father:
  - Don't call your brothers or sisters bad names; instead, just say "zak zak" (meaning smarty pants), even when you mean donkey
  - There is good and bad in everyone; take the good and leave the bad
  - We are all on the same ship in the middle of the ocean and need to keep it afloat.

- From my mother:
  - An Arabic proverb that lies don't last, "A lie's rope is short," meaning you can reach the end of the rope to the truth eventually.

In the quiet corridors of my childhood, Islamic studies emerged as a beacon of gentle wisdom, a subject woven into our school days from the tender age of five. Delivered in Arabic under the watchful eye of the Ministry of Education, it painted a portrait of a Muslim life rooted in kindness and community. We learned to cherish our surroundings—not littering in parks, greeting neighbours with a heartfelt "salamu alaikum," and steering clear of wrongdoing. The curriculum sketched the ideal believer as chaste and compassionate, warning against "rifak al sou'e" or bad companions who might lead us astray. Intrigued by this notion, I turned to my father one evening, my young mind grappling with the idea of judgement. "Who are these bad friends, Baba?" I asked, unable to fathom labelling my playmates so harshly. His response, delivered with the calm assurance that always anchored me, reshaped my world: "People are a blend of good and bad, my dear. One might smile warmly and care for their siblings, yet struggle with overeating or a harmful habit like smoking. It's for you to discern—to embrace the light and gently release the shadows." In that moment, he taught me not to condemn but to appreciate the multifaceted humanity in everyone. This lesson would later illuminate my path as Ilyas's mother, helping me see his autism not as a flaw, but a unique hue in his vibrant soul.

However, this harmony contrasted sharply with the stormier rhythms of my mother's influence. She meant the world to us, her intentions a fierce flame of love, but her voice often thundered like desert winds, laced with frustration and unyielding expectations. Perfection was her creed—an elusive ideal that cast long shadows over our home, stressing us all out in its pursuit. My brothers and I learned to tiptoe around truths, hiding mishaps or fibbing to evade her scoldings, not out of deceit, but from the raw fear of her disappointment. Her sharp and unrelenting words faded quickly from memory, while my father's serene guidance lingered like a soothing balm. Perhaps her perfectionism was a delusion we all suffered, a relentless drive that blurred the beauty of imperfection. It wasn't until grade seven that I glimpsed a different way forward, through a friendship that would redefine my approach to effort and achievement.

She boarded the school bus one crisp morning, a girl from my class whose quiet diligence had escaped my notice until then. As I passed her seat, she invited me to sit, revealing her homework with a smile—and a backup copy she'd prepared, just in case. "Wow," I thought, awestruck by her foresight. We became inseparable, our bond forged in shared bus rides and whispered conversations, even as teachers separated us to curb our chatter. From her, I absorbed the art of proactive study—tackling homework during commutes or in those fleeting minutes between classes. No longer delaying tasks, I transformed from a middling student to one who ranked first in grade nine's first term. My friends rejoiced, having seen the high scores accumulate, but joy eluded me. Instead, panic gripped my heart: Mother's pride would morph into an ironclad expectation, chaining me to endless study for the years ahead. The weight of that invisible yoke nearly broke me, a poignant reminder of how unchecked demands can stifle a child's spirit.

Reflecting on these formative years, I see parenting not as a confined role awakened only by childbirth, but as a timeless skill set causing ripples far beyond the home. We needn't wait for children to hone these abilities, which apply seamlessly to the corporate world—training teams, mediating conflicts, nurturing client relationships. At its core, effective parenting rejects superiority, viewing children not as lesser beings but as noble equals, created by God with inherent dignity. Spoon-feeding obedience erodes connection; instead, we must meet them at eye level, much like colleagues or friends. This parity mirrors leadership dynamics, where empathy and guidance foster collaboration. Indeed, research affirms that mothers often excel in such arenas:[iv] working mothers are rated superior in multitasking (63% versus 37% for others) and time management (56% versus 44%).[v] They infuse workplaces with empathy, efficiency, and resilience—qualities honed in the crucible of motherhood. As I raise Ilyas, these insights guide me to advocate for an inclusive society, where neurodivergent children like him are seen not as anomalies to fix, but as equals whose unique perspectives enrich us all.

Clashing Styles: The Dance of Discipline and Empathy

Parenting unfurls as a labyrinth of trials, where the most poignant confrontations often arise from the divergent rhythms between father and mother—each a mirror of their own upbringing, each convinced their melody is the truest. In many households, fathers linger on the periphery during those tender early years, stepping into the spotlight only as children reach five or seven, their maturity a silent cue for involvement. This shift, too, bends to gender's subtle sway: sons draw paternal guidance sooner, moulded into resilience, while daughters may drift toward maternal orbits. My own bond with my father bloomed brightest in those dawn years, up to six, when he was my world—our walks through Abu Dhabi's unhurried streets a symphony of simple joys. We wandered markets hand in hand, bantering with shopkeepers, bargaining fiercely only to circle back with triumphant tales of better deals. Parks became our sanctuaries: I skipped with wild abandon while he reclined in quiet repose, stealing moments of rest amid the burdens of providing. He was my anchor of calm, a counterpoint to my mother's whirlwind energy—the superwoman who shouldered all, her unyielding standards a double-edged sword that carved deep grooves of expectation into our lives, stressing us in ways unseen.

Paternal love, in its essence, wields the firm hand of discipline, while maternal affection flows as an unconditional river, forgiving and enveloping. My brothers perceived our parents through a different lens, their upbringing laced with lessons tailored for sons, just as mine was shaped for a daughter. Blending our worlds, my husband and I carried a mosaic of influences—Jordanian rigor, French logic, Emirati warmth, Lebanese vibrancy—into our union, a fusion destined to create sparks. Clashes were inevitable, igniting over the simplest exchanges, revealing the chasm between his structured resolve and my intuitive grace.

One recent evening etched this divide in stark relief: as we gathered in the living room, Ilyas tugged at his father's hand, remote in grasp, yearning for his beloved dog cartoon. My husband, embodying the disciplinarian, insisted on words: "Say what you want." Silence. "Ilyas, use words!" On the third command, Ilyas murmured "dog," but it wasn't enough—"Say it properly: I want to watch dog." The exchange dragged on, a battle of wills: "I wan," Ilyas echoed faintly; "Louder," came the retort. From the kitchen, chopping vegetables amid the sizzle of dinner, I listened with a sinking heart—how condescending it sounded, this insistence on perfection from a child whose world brimmed with unspoken hurdles. Ilyas, strong-willed and sensitive, met authority with defiance, what others might label stubbornness. Later, I broached it gently: "Try a softer tone—'Bravo! Say it louder?'" He bristled defensively and I relented, respecting his paternal path. Yet, the power of language lingered in my mind—words, tone, cadence—all weapons or bridges in communicating with neurodivergent souls like our son's, where a harsh edge of criticism could shatter fragile trust.

Another clash unfolded over dinner at a lavish restaurant, a rare escape I guarded fiercely. Outings with Ilyas were my domain—solo travels to Qatar and Lebanon, Dubai's intensive therapies, endless playdates and meals—where I'd learned to let him roam, scooter in tow, his transitional chariot from stroller days. That night, on the balcony overlooking the sea's shimmering expanse, with Abu Dhabi's lights twinkling like distant stars, Ilyas fidgeted, eager to scoot amid the open space. I encouraged it, knowing his harmless wanderings brought him joy. But my husband intervened, firm: "Sit down—he'll bump into tables, disturb others." Tension crackled as Ilyas resisted, the evening fracturing into a tug-of-war. "Let him play," I urged, "he'll surprise you with his care." Unmoved, he held fast, and I retreated to my meal, heart heavy, watching father and son locked in silent discord while the waves whispered below. In that moment, our styles collided—his caution a shield, mine a leash loosened by faith in Ilyas's innate sensibility.

Yet, in this interplay of contrasts, we find equilibrium: his discipline tempers my leniency, nurturing a balance that fosters resilience, independence, and unconditional love. For in the crucible of these clashes, we raise not just our son, but ourselves—crafting a family resilient enough to challenge society's norms, where neurodivergence blooms as a strength, not a shadow.

Potty Training: The Wisdom of a Mother's Intuition Over Clinical Mandates

In the early days of guiding my son toward greater independence, I approached a key developmental milestone in personal hygiene with the hopeful enthusiasm of a first-time mother. Equipped with engaging tools designed to make the process fun and rewarding, I even modelled the steps myself, sharing light-hearted moments to encourage him along. Yet, as time stretched from months into years, this seemingly straightforward phase became a profound exercise in patience, flexibility, and recognising the boundaries of expert guidance. My son, with his distinctive neurodivergent perspective, embraced this journey on his own terms, achieving some elements swiftly while others unfolded more gradually, far beyond the schedules outlined in standard parenting resources.

From his early years onward, we explored a meandering path: introducing concepts through consistent routines, using verbal cues and visual aids in various environments—home, outings, and new spaces—to build familiarity and confidence. By around age three and a half, structured behavioural therapy at home proved invaluable, emphasising steady encouragement and viewing setbacks as opportunities for growth. He practised without familiar supports during those sessions, and though challenges arose often, they fuelled real advancement. When he transitioned to school at four, his dedicated support aide (LSA#2) became a crucial partner, reading his subtle signals and adapting the setting to nurture his progress. Now, well into his fifth year, he often navigates these moments independently, a subtle victory that swells my heart with deep gratitude.

Still, certain aspects proved elusive, leading specialists to recommend occupational therapy to explore potential sensory sensitivities. Behavioural experts and their teams suggested it could address underlying discomforts, like environmental aversions (wet surroundings) or coordination hurdles (difficulty squatting into a seated position)—factors such as unease with instability or unfamiliar sensations. In our initial meeting, the therapist proposed familiar introductory strategies we'd long since moved past, prompting me to share our history gently; my son had grown and evolved, requiring approaches that matched his current capabilities. As we discussed further, she acknowledged with a knowing nod that the referral might stem more from standard protocol than a precise fit—a candid moment that highlighted the weight of our experience. It revealed a broader pattern: professionals, guided by frameworks and studies, sometimes approach complexities as procedural items, referring them onward without the intimate, day-to-day insight that parents live and breathe.

This realisation deepened a conviction I've come to hold dear: mothers possess an intuition that often outshines formal expertise. Our understanding is rooted in the raw essence of caregiving—sleepless vigils, gut feelings, and the timeless wisdom shared among generations of parents in quiet, supportive exchanges. It's pure and uncompromised, free from the influences of metrics or partnerships that can shape industries, from healthcare providers favouring certain treatments to institutions prioritising quotas, or even historical missteps like mid-century endorsements of harmful habits. Throughout my path, I've consulted a series of specialists, from initial diagnosticians to global voices through virtual communities, yet most brushed aside my questions about holistic factors like nutrition, prioritising behavioural interventions, with other elements deemed minor. Only one physician, during an exploration of alternative therapies like hyperbaric oxygen, truly engaged. He delved into my experiences, from pregnancy and early milestones to daily habits, and opened up about how similar adjustments helped his own child. His authenticity, forged from personal trials, validated my instincts: no standardised approach can fully encompass the individuality of neurodivergence, where each path resists a one-size-fits-all remedy.

Empowering parents means honouring this inherent knowledge, blending it with the communal bonds that contemporary life has sometimes weakened. Dependence on specialists has grown as families have become more self-contained, but I've learned to sift their input through the lens of my unbreakable connection with my son. Behavioural support has been a helpful thread in our tapestry, yet pauses in therapy brought subtle reminders that enduring progress blooms from a wholehearted approach—encompassing nourishment, consistency, and, most vitally, a parent's attuned presence. I've nurtured my own growth in nurturing him, calling for a society that values such parental insight, where neurodivergence isn't merely a case for experts to shuffle, but a collective narrative enriched by the wisdom of those who know their children best. For in trusting our inner guidance, we not only shepherd our little ones but light the way toward true inclusion, celebrating every unique strength as a shared treasure.

Parenting is a Concept For All, Whether Starting a Family or a Company

Parenting transcends the confines of family life, extending its profound wisdom to realms as diverse as founding a company or leading a team. It equips us with timeless principles for human connection, which resonate far beyond the nursery walls.

Consider the art of resolving discord among colleagues: when viewpoints clash or corrections meet resistance, wise leaders counsel a measured retreat—first to foster open dialogue, then further still to cultivate genuine rapport. This mirrors the sacred rhythm of early childhood, where the initial seven years are devoted not to admonition but to forging unbreakable bonds. In those formative moments, children explore the world with unbridled curiosity, oblivious to perils or societal judgements; premature attempts to curtail their instincts risk fracturing trust. Just as we must meet our young ones with patience and presence, so too must we approach our professional counterparts, allowing relationships to bloom before imposing change.

Similarly, the emphasis on nurturing strengths unites the spheres of home and work. Parents are wise to celebrate their child's innate gifts—be it a passion for a single sport, an academic pursuit, or an artistic flair—rather than demanding mastery in all. Specialisation, after all, breeds excellence. In the corporate arena, this translates to feedback that begins with affirmation, highlighting competencies before gently addressing areas for growth, or assigning roles that align with an individual's unique talents. Through such parallels, parenting emerges not merely as a duty but as a masterclass in empathy and elevation. When applied broadly, it weaves the fabric of an inclusive society—where neurodivergent individuals like my son are not moulded to fit arbitrary norms, but empowered to shine in their authenticity, enriching us all.

Concluding this chapter on parenting, we embrace the diverse styles of being a mother or father, recognising that they need not align perfectly. Cultural clashes, far from being obstacles, invite us to experiment with love and patience. Parenting is learned through trial and error, not rigid rules. I've come to see that "right and wrong" are often unyielding labels, inherited from tradition or expectation, that can stifle the unique needs of our children. Instead, I focus on "good and bad"—actions that nurture connection, reduce harm, and foster growth. The bar of goodness for society lies in what I can justify to a child: choices that build trust, honour individuality, and weave a compassionate, inclusive world where every soul belongs.

The next chapter will discuss the outcome of a couple bringing a child into the world: the family.

3

WHAT IS A FAMILY?

Crafting the Bedrock of an Inclusive Society

"It takes a village to raise a child," the proverb declares, yet today we must "raise a village to raise a child." In a world of fading connections, my journey raising Ilyas, an autistic child, revealed the family's vital role in weaving values that shape inclusive societies.

The family plays a vital role in society, which largely caters to families. What happens in the family, from parenting to communicating to instilling values, shapes our future generations. A family that values honesty will produce adults who conduct work in an honest manner and diminish instances of fraud at the corporate level. This chapter will tell the story of how I valued my family's advice above doctors' opinions, how my family extends to nannies and shadow teacher roles (also known as Learning Support Assistants (LSAs)), and how my family engages with wider society, providing feedback to improve society's services.

The Breaking Dawn: Facing the Shadow of Diagnosis

The revelation that my son Ilyas carried the weight of autism did not crash upon me but seeped in gradually, a slow-dawning eclipse shrouding my heart in layers of denial, flickering curiosity, and suffocating overwhelm. It began innocently enough, with internet searches that spiralled into a labyrinth of global remedies—promises of cures from distant shores, tangled theories on causes that only deepened the fog of uncertainty. By the time we sought formal answers, Ilyas was nearing three, his world a mosaic of therapies that had become our fragile lifeline.

We had been loyal to Clinic #2, its halls a familiar battleground for speech and occupational sessions. But the doctor's initial nudge toward assessment in August 2022 met my resolute "no"—a shield against the unknown. By October, doubt crept in, but she was then departing, leaving us adrift. Whispers led us to a renowned neurodevelopmental specialist at Hospital #1, his name synonymous with hope. That afternoon's appointment was a tempest in miniature: Ilyas, robbed of his nap, unravelled in tantrums—first a wail on the road, then chaos at the supermarket as I desperately soothed his cries. By the time we spilled into the office, we were a whirlwind—I pushing his stroller like a weary nomad, Ilyas flinging a chewed ball of yarn skyward in defiant arcs, his frustration mirroring my own exhaustion.

The doctor wasted no breath on pleasantries. "Your son is autistic—severely so," he declared, his words slicing through the air like a sharpened blade. Fatigue dulled my shock; I managed only a weary smile, thinking, "Was it so evident, this invisible veil over my child?" We retraced our path: the cocktail of occupational therapy (OT), speech therapy (ST), and behavioural glimpses through ABA (intensive behavioural therapy). He nodded, then pivoted: "Speech won't penetrate until his behaviour is reined in. An autistic child can't grasp instructions amid chaos—he won't mimic, won't focus, won't even meet the therapist's gaze." It resonated; Ilyas ignored his name, disregarded pointed fingers, fled any seat after mere moments. Yet I clung to memories of his earlier self—at eighteen months, he'd halt when we cried "Stop" in marching play, point to animals in books, beam with eye contact that now felt like a distant dream. Perhaps that nostalgia fuelled my delay, a mother's desperate grip on "normalcy".

Four exhausting evaluation sessions followed with another specialist, each a battlefield of Ilyas's resistance and my silent pleas. At last, both doctors convened with me, their plan a decree: "Educate yourself on autism. Register him as a Student of Determination. Join parent support groups." But the core thrust was ABA, heralded as the golden key. "It's the only path," they insisted, their voices a chorus of urgency. My spirit rebelled. "I can't afford it," I countered, the words tasting like ash. They arched eyebrows, incredulous—an Emirati mother, pleading poverty? But reality bit hard: our insurance covered only ST and OT, not this "essential" lifeline. Intensive meant twenty-five hours weekly—a fortune, yes, but more than money, it demanded time. When would Ilyas breathe, play, simply *be*? "You're suggesting clinics over nurseries?" I challenged. "Robbing him of peers for sterile sessions?"

Their insistence reached a crescendo, crashing like a wave against my resolve. But in that sterile room, amid charts and clinical detachment, a fire ignited within me—a mother's unyielding sovereignty. "No," I declared, my voice steady as the desert sands. "The best treatment for my son isn't what you prescribe—it's what our family deems right. I'll consult his father, his grandmother, our kin. This isn't just financial; it's our minds, our bodies, our souls. Even if we muster the funds and clear his days, who drives him through the endless commutes? Who holds the fragments of our lives together?"

In that defiant stand, emotion surged—tears unshed, a heart torn between fear and fierce love. Autism wasn't a foe to conquer with regimens alone; it was a journey demanding holistic wisdom, where family voices drowned out expert edicts. For in blindly following orders, we risk erasing the child's essence; but in claiming our narrative, we honour the truth that healing blooms not in isolation, but in the embrace of those who know him best.

Systemic Barriers

This was a family decision to be made, because what is best for my son is bound by his family's capacities. Yes, mothers will go out of their way to provide for their children, but what's the point if it is at the expense of their health, time, or sanity? Mothers have other duties as wives, daughters, and full-time employees to provide for all the expenses creeping up on running a household.

Many view families as isolated units responsible solely for their own, ignoring their societal role. This individualistic shift, coupled with over-reliance on clinical solutions for neurodivergent children, marginalises family wisdom. I initially trusted doctors' ABA mandates for Ilyas, only to find them costly (AED 400 per hour) and impractical, reflecting society's tendency to prioritise experts over parental input. The belief that families can function in silos dismisses their power to shape equitable communities, leaving neurodivergent children vulnerable to systemic barriers.

The family is society's bedrock, weaving values like honesty and compassion into future generations. Extending to caregivers like LSAs, families must advocate for their children while prioritising collective wellbeing by serving the community. In our case, this meant valuing family consensus over clinical demands, seeing Ilyas's autism as a strength. This perspective positions families as active builders of inclusive societies, where service and advocacy dissolve barriers including prejudice and isolation.

Although three-generational households once fostered unity in Emirati culture, modern nuclear families risk disconnection. This disconnect has magnified the lens on neurodivergent symptoms of autism and ADHD since children are missing the care of close family members (grandparents, aunts and uncles, cousins of their own age) and are in the strange care of hired nannies, or the supervised watch of a driver in his/her spare time, or the afterschool support of a Learning Support Assistant. My appeals to Abu Dhabi's government hotline about nursery policies revealed the gaps that burden nuclear families, forcing reliance on external caregivers. I questioned why hiring a stranger, possibly newly arrived from abroad, was deemed acceptable, while training a trusted family member (such as my young cousin) with a 40-hour behavioural analysis course to serve as Ilyas's LSA was dismissed. Our experience with LSA #1, who neglected Ilyas's potty training by deferring to assistants, highlighted the pitfalls of outsourcing care to those who may not share our family's values. Families, as society's cornerstone, must reclaim their role in making informed decisions for their children, ensuring caregivers align with the cultural and emotional bonds that strengthen both home and community.

The Family as the Foundation of Society

The family is the cornerstone of any society, not a standalone entity but the very heart of human connection. Each of us belongs to a family, and through it, we are woven into the fabric of our community. The strength of an individual, a family, and a society are intertwined—when one thrives, so do the others, bound by a shared commitment to collective wellbeing.

The Family as a Nursery for Values and Skills

At the heart of every thriving society lies the family, that sacred cradle where human virtues and aptitudes first take root—a primordial academy shaping resilient souls equipped to face life's tempests with grace and empathy. Here, amid the intimate rhythms of daily life, we instil habits of love, patience, fairness, and justice, virtues that ripple outward, influencing our conduct in boardrooms, neighbourhoods, civic forums, and the global stage. The art of forging authentic bonds with others is honed in these formative years, within the family's tender embrace. Yet the family risks becoming a fracture in the social fabric if we overlook this vital role in nurturing cooperation, unity, and harmonious coexistence, unravelling the very bonds that sustain us.

In our Emirati culture, this nurturing extends naturally to those who share our hearth, like nannies who become woven into the household's tapestry. For my autistic son, Ilyas, their understanding was paramount, a bridge to his world of unspoken needs. Thus, the nannies who graced our home were granted afternoons free from household drudgery, devoted instead to him. Thrice weekly, as the ABA therapist arrived to weave behavioural threads into his days, the nanny was invited to observe, inquire, and absorb—a deliberate path to enrich her interactions and deepen her knowledge. In theory, it was flawless: a symphony of growth where her evolving insights would harmonise with Ilyas's progress. I monitored closely, one nanny at a time—from the first in the spring of 2023 to the second that autumn—offering written guidance and hands-on coaching.

Yet, each nanny faltered at the core: missing the essence that Ilyas must not grow overly dependent, that patience was their shield against his clever manipulations. Their shortcomings, compounded by unreliability and cost, led me to release them and manage household chores independently within my family members. After all, a revolving door of caregivers might teach my son that people are fleeting presences, eroding his grasp on enduring relationships. Moreover, we already had a steadfast guardian in his school shadow teacher, rendering further home support redundant.

WHAT IS A FAMILY?

The shadow teacher transcended her role—she became an extension of our family, a vital link in society's chain, linking Ilyas's home sanctuary with the wider world of learning. She was the conduit between our intimate routines and the classroom's bustle, and I held sacred the bond she forged with him, just as I nurtured my own with her. We had extended the same generosity to our nannies, only to see it exploited; whispers branded me "too kind," but I refused to dim my essence to counter another's shortcomings.

Drawing from my behavioural analysis training, I knew the foundation lay in "pairing"—that initial dance of child-led play to build trust. Thus, when we welcomed our first Learning Support Assistant (LSA #1) in July 2023, I insisted she spend an hour each afternoon with Ilyas, to weave familiarity before the academic year dawned. This was amid the storm: Nursery #3, where he'd summered since 2022, decreed he could not return without her, thrusting us into a hunt for this elusive ally. No regulatory body governed them; no ready pool of candidates awaited; direction was scarce.

A Facebook post went forth: "Seeking a shadow teacher trained in behavioural therapy for an autistic three-year-old at nursery—energetic for outdoor play, clear in communication, as he understands all yet speaks none. Hours: 7:30 a.m. to 2:00 p.m. in [Location]."

Applications flooded in, a deluge of mismatches: a man proxying for his wife (a red flag of ineptitude), foreigners craving visas, distant seekers demanding sponsorship and lodging. They seemed blind to the heart of my plea—the autistic child. Exhausted by the barrage of inadequate replies, I dialled my trusted lifeline: Abu Dhabi's government toll-free number, a therapeutic outlet for grievances turned productive. They documented my plight, routing it to education regulators who clarified policies: schools capped fees for Students of Determination (SOD) at 150% of standard tuition, but nurseries danced to their own tune. "What of the added LSA salary atop that?" I pressed, decrying the 300% burden compared to neurotypical families. Their counsel: persist via social media or switch nurseries if exploited. Reluctant to uproot Ilyas yet again, I resolved to endure at Nursery #3, redoubling efforts to secure a worthy LSA.

Guidance flowed from unexpected quarters: a respected colleague, a behaviourist I admired, unveiled agencies specialising in shadow teacher curation—pools of trained professionals matched to children's needs. Promising yet prohibitive, with salaries beginning at AED 7,000. Undeterred, I consulted our original BCBA, who furnished CVs. Interviews ensued—phone screenings, home visits where candidates engaged Ilyas, immersing themselves in our world. We chose LSA #1, who shone in her audition, pledging aid in speech and potty training as school loomed. If only we'd glimpsed her duplicity then: she concealed her aversion to diaper duties before shirking them entirely, inflicting unseen harm that surfaced months later.

WHAT IS A FAMILY?

The ache lingers as I reflect: how fervently I championed her, only to be met with self-serving deceit. She phoned at midday on her inaugural nursery day, decrying the chaos and incessant music. Though I liaised daily with teachers and played in the playground during drop-offs (being barred from classrooms as a parent), I validated her concerns, prioritising Ilyas's comfort. I withdrew him by day two, confronting administration in a resolute twenty-minute exchange reminding them of my growing concerns since summer that their teachers always managed to dismiss swiftly, but are now materialising with the LSA's similar concerns. They disparaged the LSA's view. "I choose her now," I countered, having already invested eight weeks in her bond with my son—one she later betrayed by delegating his care during vulnerable moments. This defence recurred at his first school, her flaws amplified without assistants to mask them. Aides at Nursery #4 handled toddlers' needs, concealing her neglect; she excelled in behavioural cues—queuing, turn-taking, sustained focus—and speech prompts, her lanyards featuring a trio of flashcards for nouns, verbs, and sequences. Yet, beneath it all, her refusal to engage in potty training festered.

We launched the year at Nursery #3, only to pivot by day four to a fresh, organically harmonious haven with LSA #1. That month, Ilyas regressed: dry nights vanished, replaced by leaks soaking his pyjamas and sheets. My intuition whispered of a cause amid the flux: a new nursery yes, but one where he thrived as I witnessed in my morning play sessions, or was it LSA #1, yet she was familiar since July.

Clarity dawned in January 2024: a message from her, summoning me mid-work to change his soiled diaper. The pieces shattered into truth—she had evaded this duty, pushing him to aides, her lies a veil concealing harm. My heart fractured anew in that betrayal, a mother's fierce protectiveness clashing with the trust I'd bestowed. Yet it reaffirmed a deeper lesson: extending family to such roles demands rigorous training, unwavering evaluation, and trust earned through deeds, not words. For in society's grand weave, these extensions—nannies, shadow teachers—are threads that must align with our values, fostering not just care, but the enduring compassion that binds us all, neurodivergent and beyond, in an inclusive embrace.

The Family's Duty to Serve the Common Good

While the family tenderly cultivates the wellbeing of its own members, its enduring power resides in its profound calling as a societal pillar, steadfastly committed to collective flourishing. Far from an insular haven, the family's essence radiates outward, enriching the broader community and upholding its role as society's foundational stone. It was in this spirit of outreach that, following the doctor's solemn confirmation of my son's autism—now articulated through nuance rather than stark labels like "severe" or "mild"—I returned home, my heart heavy yet resolute, to engage in a heartfelt dialogue with my husband. Their recommendations lingered in my mind like echoes in a vast chamber: intensive therapies, structured

WHAT IS A FAMILY?

supports, a path forward fraught with uncertainty. I seized upon them, devoting hours to the digital expanse, dialling contacts unearthed from online listings, driven by a mother's unyielding love to forge connections that might illuminate our way.

Among the resources they offered were two lifelines: a parents' support group for those navigating the spectrum, and an institute specialising in training and deploying Registered Behaviour Technicians for home-based care. The support group's website gleamed with promise—pages brimming with information, a beacon in the fog of isolation. Yet its interactivity proved illusory; after navigating its pages, I stumbled upon membership tiers and, with a flicker of hope, enrolled at the modest fee of AED 120. I anticipated a response, a human touch—perhaps a call, an email, even an automated nod of acknowledgment. Days blurred into weeks as I scoured my inbox and spam folders, my anticipation curdling into quiet despair, the silence amplifying the loneliness of our journey. It felt like a void, a digital echo of the societal gaps that so often swallow families like ours, leaving us adrift in a sea of unanswered questions.

Fate intervened two months later, in the unlikeliest of settings: my workplace. A colleague, privy to fragments of my story through our candid exchanges, mentioned an impending meeting with the group's founder and CEO. As her words stirred a storm within me, my immediate retort was laced with bitterness: "It must be a scam." The absence of any follow-up had eroded my trust, evoking the raw vulnerability of a mother grasping for solidarity only to clasp empty air. Yet she addressed my doubts with empathy, furnishing the CEO's email for direct pursuit. That professional rendezvous held such potential; she yearned to champion my perspective as an end-user, ensuring authenticity before our organisation entwined with this advocacy entity. In that moment, a spark of communal hope reignited, reminding me that families like mine are not solitary islands but vital threads in society's fabric—our outreach, our persistence, a quiet revolution toward realising an inclusive world where neurodivergent children like Ilyas are embraced, not overlooked, and where the common good becomes a shared, unbreakable bond.

The Power of Service in Strengthening Society

A family that embraces its role as a societal cornerstone naturally turns outward, attuned to the needs of its community and eager to contribute. Service is more than an act—it's a way of being, a heartfelt drive to give without expecting anything in return. This quality fuels progress in ever-evolving societies. Individuals exercise their agency through service, actively shaping their communities for the better. When families serve together, they forge bonds of friendship and camaraderie, united by a shared purpose. This collective effort dissolves barriers like prejudice or isolation, weaving a stronger, more cohesive society, no matter how diverse its members. Service, rooted in the family, becomes a bridge to unity and an antidote to loneliness.

Embracing the Ripple: Families as Catalysts for Societal Harmony

Families have increasingly retreated into their own sanctuaries, each unit a self-contained island adrift in a sea of disconnection. In our modern lives, it's become all too common to declare, "Each neighbour to their own," a sentiment that feels alien to the warmth of our cultural heritage. I recall the days when we would linger outside our homes, exchanging smiles and greetings with every passerby, or slip plates of homemade sweets to a neighbour's door as a quiet gesture of care. Our children roamed freely together, their laughter echoing through shared play, while our men gathered in the local mosque for prayers, forging bonds in sacred unity. These simple rituals wove us into a vibrant community tapestry, one thread strengthening the next.

Yet, imperceptibly, those threads began to fray. Today, even our men seek distant mosques, evading the familiar faces that once offered solace, as if proximity itself has become a burden. I remember a quiet evening when my father gently asked me to park my white car around the back of the house, away from prying eyes. He spared me the full tale, but I later pieced it together: neighbours had noted my late returns, their whispers brewing into gossip that could tarnish our family's peace.

He taught me the sting of surveillance in shielding me from judgement, but it left a deeper ache—the erosion of trust that once bound us.

Is this the root of our withdrawal, this fear of gossip's venomous bite? Undoubtedly, idle talk poisons any haven, yet in fleeing it, we inflict a greater wound: the unravelling of our societal cohesion. If families are indeed the bedrock of civilisation—each one a brick in the grand edifice—how then can we reclaim the art of loving interaction? For families like mine, raising a neurodivergent child, this isolation cuts deepest; it denies us the communal embrace that could transform challenges into shared triumphs. In rediscovering our outward gaze, we not only heal our neighbourhoods but nurture an inclusive world, where every soul, visible in their struggles or hidden in their strengths, finds belonging in the collective heart.

As we conclude this section, we learnt the value of a child in a family and the role of parents. While parents will do anything for their children, the best option is that which not only serves the child but the family as a whole. The family—parents, their children, their extended relatives, and their domestic helpers (nannies, drivers, housekeepers)—make up the building blocks of their society. Dysfunctional families will make up for chaotic unorganised societies. Families that do not apply virtues in their core practices will inflict harm within themselves. Globally, the rates of Autism Spectrum Disorder (ASD) and Attention Deficit Hyperactivity Disorder (ADHD) are on the rise. While many causes are being studied, the family's composition is a decisive factor, since the family is a child's first home and shelter after their mother's womb. So, how do we maintain sane families that connect with each other and converse with their societies? This will be discussed in the next section: practising.

SECTION 2:

PRACTISING

In this pivotal section, I turn our gaze to the tangible artistry of parenting—the deliberate practices that transform intention into action, and how they yield profound rewards for both caregiver and child. We begin with Chapter 4 on the art of observing, followed by Chapter 5 on sensing, and culminate in Chapter 6 on reflecting. These are not mere techniques but essential personal attributes, ones that every individual—whether as a mother, a father, a teacher, or simply a fellow human engaging with children and others—must cultivate to deepen their relational wisdom.

No guidebook or sage can fully equip you for the sacred odyssey of parenthood; it unfolds as a singular path, etched uniquely for each of us. Yet, in committing to daily practice—indeed, tailoring it to every fleeting encounter with your child or those in your care—we unlock opportunities to elevate our connections, infusing them with grace and understanding. Reflection stands as the cornerstone of these habits, a universal imperative woven into the fabric of our lives. Even in adolescence, our faith gently beckons us to ponder our deeds during moments of prayer, fostering a lifelong rhythm of introspection. The companion practices of sensing and observing assume heightened urgency when nurturing children on the spectrum or with diverse abilities, for they often navigate worlds where words fall short, compelling us to attune to subtle precursors of their behaviours. Neurodivergent souls, like my beloved Ilyas, may harbour exquisite sensitivities that elude casual notice; it falls to us—their guardians, peers, and society—to comprehend these nuances, bridging divides with empathy that honours their experiences in every shared moment. In doing so, we not only support them but weave a more compassionate tapestry for all, where inclusion is not an aspiration but a lived reality.

4

AM I OBSERVANT?

Observing my environment is regulating my inner feelings

When was the last time you were doing a task and let yourself take all the time it needed, instead of rushing it or thinking about a faster way to complete the task at hand? Being present in the moment, the here and now, is giving every task, every situation, every person their rightful worth.

By the end of this chapter, you will realise that connecting with children and people starts simply by practising observation. Observation was a given decades ago when people had no distractions. Now—due to our smartphones pinging frequently, our paths flashing with billboards, our spaces buzzing with music and announcements—we need to learn how to observe.

The Echoes of Presence: Navigating Disconnection in a Fast-Paced World

In the intimate dance of motherhood with my autistic son, every fleeting glance, every subtle shift in his expression, feels like a lifeline I dare not overlook—yet, in truth, I miss so many. Our modern world hurtles forward at a relentless pace, besieged by gadgets and media that invade not just our physical spaces but the quiet corners of our minds, leaving us fragmented and adrift. How often do we nod absently through a conversation, our thoughts ensnared in an endless cascade of tasks, mentally checking boxes while the person before us fades into the background? This detachment seeps into every bond—not only with our children, whose worlds we long to inhabit fully, but with our partners, friends, and colleagues—propelling us through life on autopilot, where human presence is a rare luxury.

Yet forging a profound connection with our little ones, especially those navigating the intricate landscapes of neurodivergence, demands more than mere proximity; it calls for an unwavering commitment to the now, a presence that can feel elusive amid the chaos. Those ephemeral moments, when captured wholly, work quiet miracles in a child's soul—they blossom with the assurance of being truly seen, heard, and cherished. Contrary to the myth that such attunement requires superhuman vigour or impeccable parenting, it asks only for a subtle awakening: the recognition of those invisible rifts in our interactions, the hidden currents of disconnection that erode our ties. With one intentional shift—a pause to truly observe—we unlock transformations that ripple outward, mending not just our familial threads but weaving a more empathetic society where neurodivergent voices like Ilyas's are no longer overlooked, but honoured as essential harmonies in our shared human symphony.

The Art of Attunement: Decoding the Layers of Environment and Emotion

To cultivate true observance, one must attune to the multi-faceted layers of the environment and the individual within it. This encompasses a comprehensive scan of external factors—the prevailing weather, ambient noise levels, illumination, olfactory cues, and even air quality—each of which can subtly influence mood and behaviour, particularly in neurodivergent children whose sensory processing may amplify such elements. Beyond the surroundings, extend this vigilance to the child themselves, endeavouring to infer their internal state by empathising deeply: not merely stepping into their shoes, but inhabiting their thoughts, their physical sensations, even their subtle bodily signals.

One evening after dinner, for instance, as Ilyas contentedly with his toys in our living room, I presented a plate of mandarin segments, knowing his fondness for the fruit. He approached and sat beside me, yet instead of reaching for a piece, he emitted a soft whine—a non-verbal expression of his inner world. Perplexed by his apparent discontent, I paused to reflect: he had just enjoyed a hearty meal of mashed potatoes and ground beef, so I imagined myself in his position, feeling satiated yet tempted by the citrus aroma. Concluding he might simply be too full to partake, I set the plate aside and reassured him gently that he could enjoy it later, when his appetite returned. This moment, though seemingly minor, underscored the power of such attunement.

One might perceive this level of scrutiny as overly meticulous, yet it is essential for fostering independence in children, provided there exists a robust channel of communication between the young learner and their guiding adult. Children absorb knowledge with remarkable rapidity, necessitating caregivers to validate or gently correct their emerging understandings along the way. For neurodivergent children, however, this exchange is often more nuanced—not solely due to limited verbal expression or reliance on visual aids, but because of their distinct sensory profiles, which can render everyday stimuli profoundly impactful. The depth of our engagements with our children transcends surface-level offerings; it would become effortless to remain fully present and discern these cues if we merely decelerated our pace, resisting the siren call of life's myriad distractions that so often pull us from the richness of the moment. In embracing this practice, we not only honour the unique needs of individuals like Ilyas but also model a more empathetic framework for society, where inclusion arises from mindful awareness rather than oversight.

Embracing Positivity in Perception: Practical Pathways to Observant Parenting

Being observant may be accomplished by having a positive perspective on the situation. While being observant implies caution and premeditation, this will influence the situation with negative energy. Conversely, positively engaging with your child involves providing the required attention in the right space, providing the safety and happiness your child needs.

One example is playing with your child when you take them out to a play area or playground instead of just watching over them. While playing with other children, some areas might not fit your adult size, so do whatever fits you. That is a simple shift in attitude from a responsible adult watching over their child (willing them not to trip, not to hurt others, not to chew on toys) to playing along and being in the state required by the space. As your engagement as a parent becomes appropriate, the energy around you will fit with the purpose of the play.

Noticing changes in your environment or in people, such as someone's new haircut, the rearrangement of a desk in the office, or using a different tea, helps practise our observation. Having a keen eye for details allows us to absorb information which may feed into the reasons for a person's state of mind. Further skills that help in our perception include:

- Reading **body language**, from facial expressions to posture and certain gestures, can help identify a person's emotions or feelings early on so that you may tie them to any circumstantial change, or a word uttered by another person. It may seem trivial, but by observing the person we love and cherish, these intuitive natural instincts may kick in before we know it. Intuition is a mother's weapon, as it includes knowing her gut feeling is right when there is something wrong. This is a learnt practice that our subconscious builds by observing patterns.
- Sensing your **surroundings** such as temperature changes, bright lights, and new scents in the air, also helps reveal that my child's general environment may 'suddenly' affect his behaviour, removing the element of surprise.
- Often, you will be able to **sense what is not being said**, especially with a non-verbal child. This is why we practise being observant and encourage him to speak up by modelling the words for what he wants or what he feels. For some autistics, knowing their own emotions and identifying them is difficult; hence observing behaviours or changes in tone helps read emotions of the autistic child (even adults) and react better and kinder to the situation.
- With practice, observance will help predict people's behaviours and reactions. Mothers tend to predict how their child

AM I OBSERVANT?

will react based on observing their behaviours and **identifying patterns and motives**. This is sometimes done out of amusement, yet is surely helpful for situations involving autistics. So mothers, continue being you and trust your gut feelings!

- Supporting material: to aid your practice, consider this simple observation checklist template:

Observation Aspect	Details Noted	Potential Impact on Child	Action Taken
Environment (noise, light, smell)			
Body Language (posture, gestures)			
Unspoken Emotions			
Patterns Observed			
Use this table daily to log observations and review weekly. For further resources, explore blog articles on the benefits of parent observations in ABA therapy from Discovery ABA (discoveryaba.com) or the role of observational learning from Grateful Care ABA (gratefulcareaba.com). A step-by-step example: During a playground visit, note high noise levels (environment) or your child's furrowed brow (body language), link it to sensory overload, then move to a quieter area.			

The Hidden Costs of Distraction: Embracing Perception as a Hidden Path to Joyful Connection

In our whirlwind lives, it's all too easy to overlook the subtle rhythms unfolding around us, our minds ensnared by endless mental checklists or the glow of our screens, pulling us away from the present like a relentless tide. Yet cultivating observance—and evolving it into true perception—unveils a profound joy, a celebration of life's intricate details that we might otherwise dismiss as insignificant. With deliberate practice, tuning into our surroundings and the nuances of others' behaviours invites us to decelerate, savouring existence in its fuller, richer hues. It may require stepping back in social gatherings, adopting a quieter stance to absorb the ebb and flow of conversations, the unspoken dances of interaction. In this stillness we recharge, processing the raw tapestry of information before us, fostering a perception that transcends mere knowledge—it's about how we interpret and honour the world's quiet whispers, building bridges of empathy in a society that often rushes past the neurodivergent souls among us.

That truth crystallised for me on a fateful day, as I navigated the bustling streets of Abu Dhabi with my son, Ilyas, en route to an appointment with the seasoned neurodevelopmental paediatrician at Hospital #1—the very doctor who would first confirm his autism diagnosis. To ease the drive, I decided on a simple treat: a bag of fries from a nearby fast-food chain, a

AM I OBSERVANT?

rare indulgence now that Ilyas's diet has shifted toward nourishment over novelty, reserving such delights for occasional social moments. I parked across the two-lane road, the hum of traffic a constant undercurrent, and led Ilyas by the hand into the counter's warmth. Even at his young age, he recognised the intoxicating scent of sizzling oil, his eyes lighting up with anticipation as he sensed a snack on the horizon. He eagerly reached for our paper bag as I claimed it, his small fingers brushing the crinkled edges.

But innocence met reality in an instant. Back then, Ilyas hadn't yet grasped the sting of heat, insisting on a fry as we crossed back toward the car. I handed him one, hoping the touch would teach him gently. Instead, the scalding warmth forced his grip to falter, and the fry tumbled to the asphalt, landing squarely on the road. His face crumpled into a wail of pure anguish, a piercing cry that echoed his grief over this lost treasure. He pivoted, determined to reclaim it, oblivious to the cars weaving perilously close. My heart surged as I clutched him tightly, his tiny body writhing in protest. In that chaotic blur, we sank to the ground together on the unforgiving pavement, our eyes fixed on that solitary fry, just a metre away yet worlds out of reach, symbolising his shattered expectation.

Words failed me in that raw moment; I murmured reassurances about the abundance still in the bag, but his sorrow drowned them out, as if he were mourning something far deeper than a morsel of food—a profound, unspoken loss. Observing him closely, I traced the storm of emotions across his face: the furrowed brow of confusion, the quivering lip of betrayal, the rigid posture of unmet need. It was this attentive gaze, this commitment to witnessing his inner turmoil without haste, that sustained us through the commotion. I didn't rush to fix it; instead, I blew cool air over fresh fries, offering them as tangible proof that not all was lost, allowing him to process this reality in his own time. This was a hurdle Ilyas had to navigate, one where my arsenal of calming techniques—honed through countless therapies—felt distant and inadequate without practice.

Yet simply being there, a steadfast presence amid his struggle, proved enough. No gadgets or distractions; just us, grounded together. Our children, especially those like Ilyas on the autism spectrum, often crave a rock to anchor them—or, as Bryana Kappadakunnel, the Conscious Mommy, so poetically describes, a buoy in turbulent waters: "Co-regulation is when you stand in your boat and you toss out a buoy. You stay steady inside your boat, and the rope is strong enough to withstand whatever force comes against it. You offer comfort and affection as you watch your child find their way to the buoy. You prioritise listening while you pull them back into the safety of your boat, which has been minimally impacted by the storm you both just faced."

Indeed, soothing phrases abound—"I'm sorry, this is tough; I'm here, let's hug"—alongside breathing exercises or emotion flashcards that prompt a child to name their feelings. In one of Ilyas's earlier nurseries, the assistants, guided by a special needs educator, would flash an "angry" card at him during upsets, repeating the word in the hopes he'd echo it. But this only amplified his fury, a clear sign that the method missed the mark, yet some caregivers cling to rote strategies without pausing to reassess. When dysregulation surges, words often glance off like rain on stone, drowned by the roar of erupting emotions; forcing identification only heightens the chaos and bewilderment.

What truly aids the child is granting space for the storm to pass—anger, frustration, even jealousy—allowing them to rediscover their footing. As parents and caregivers, our gift is calm, patient presence, creating a sanctuary where emotions can flow freely, unjudged. In this way, we model for society an inclusive ethos: one that honours neurodivergent experiences not as aberrations to correct, but as vital threads in our collective humanity, weaving resilience and understanding into the fabric of our world.

The Criticality of Co-Regulation

As an Emirati mother, I see my child's big emotions like a sudden desert wind—wild surges of prickly dust in my eyes. Co-regulation is about being their calm shelter in that storm, like providing sunglasses to shield their eyes and holding their hand as they learn to walk in the soft sands. It's not just about teaching them how to steady themselves; it's about being there, strong and patient, until they find their own balance. When I stay calm during their tears or anger, I show them that it's okay to feel deeply. I'm telling them, with my presence, "You are safe, my heart, and I am here with you." Over time, this closeness helps their little hearts and minds learn to handle stress on their own, building strength for the future, like planting a date palm that grows tall and steady.

How to Soothe Your Child in the Moment

When my child is upset, I first turn inward, as we do before prayer, to calm my own heart. Am I breathing softly, or is my body tight with worry? To help my child, I must first find peace within myself, like the stillness of the desert at dawn. Then, I look into their eyes and name their feelings with love. If they're crying over a lost toy, I might say, "Oh, my darling, I see how much that toy means to you. Your heart is so sad." These gentle words, like a warm embrace, help ease their pain. Sometimes, the best thing is to simply sit close, letting them cry or rest in my arms, offering the quiet comfort of a mother's love, like the shade of a tree, making them feel safe and cherished.

Calming Strategies Through Observant Presence

Being a mother teaches one that every child is unique, and that different techniques would work on different children and adults too. Hence, while the tools to calming might change with different people, the most detrimental factor to calming is remaining anchored as the mother or the grown-up and being present throughout your child's dysregulated incident. Be observant and notice your child's emotions on their body, reddening of the face, confused looks of their eyes, or sudden hand movements. Sometimes my son would mimic the 'head, shoulders' dance moves (even when he was sitting down), and I realised he was doing it when anxious. So, I would gently sing the words as he moved his hands up to his head, shoulders, then down to knees and toes. At the part of the song on face parts, I would test his calmness by moving my fingers in a soft caressing stroke around eyes, ears, mouth and nose. By the time I reach 'nose' I do a little squeeze at the tip of his nose and his eyes shift to look at me with a smile. He reached a safe place knowing I am here with him. This presence—attuned, compassionate, and steady—is the greatest gift we can offer. Emotions, like waves, will rise and fall; our role is to anchor them with love, ensuring they feel safe. By watching closely—seeing their eyes dart (sight) or hearing their shaky voice (hearing)—we help their minds settle, ready to face the world again.

Tailored Tools for Soothing Young Hearts

For toddlers, sensory activities can work like magic to ease dysregulation. Encourage them to squeeze soft dough or hug a favourite stuffed toy, feeling its warmth. A burst of energy, like stomping their feet with crossed arms or letting out a playful roar, can help them release pent-up feelings, much like children chasing each other in a courtyard game. Colouring vibrant patterns can also ground them, bringing calm to their busy minds.

Older children may find peace in different ways; journaling lets them pour out their thoughts, while soft music soothes their emotions. A weighted blanket offers comforting pressure, or reading a beloved story can transport them to a quieter place. Never underestimate the power of a warm embrace or gentle rocking; human connection is a balm for overwhelm. Some children need space to breathe; others need to let their energy out. If they want to scream, guide them to a pillow. If they need to move, run a lap together in the garden. By observing their unique needs—whether they shy away from touch or crave it—you can offer the right tools to restore their calm.

Managing the Anger

In the hushed glow of a morning mall play area, where the world felt ours alone, Ilyas and I discovered a fleeting paradise of foam blocks and endless slides. At first, it was just us—his laughter echoing as he ingeniously stacked those soft bricks at the slide's base, transforming a simple descent into a triumphant cascade of tumbling towers. I positioned myself below, a silent guardian, restacking them faithfully as he looped around, his eyes alight with unbridled creativity. But as other

AM I OBSERVANT?

children trickled in, two young brothers joined the fray, their energy a gentle intrusion on our solitude. One clambered to the top before Ilyas, and in my encouragement—"Go on, slide down!"—I unwittingly shattered my son's fragile world. From his perch, Ilyas watched in horror as the boy hurtled down, scattering his meticulously built creation. What I saw as shared joy—a child's gleeful excitement—felt to him like profound betrayal, a theft of his invention by the very person sworn to protect it: me.

His face crumpled into raw anguish, a silent storm brewing in his non-verbal soul. Frustration surged—not just from the loss, but from the aching void of being misunderstood, his complex inner world trapped without words to set it free. He descended in a fury, flinging the bricks skyward, one grazing the younger brother in a moment that pierced my heart like a dagger. Panic gripped me; I whispered "bismillah," invoking divine calm as I tried to guide him away, shielding others from his whirlwind. But Ilyas, dysregulated and adrift, resisted every touch—kicking, swaying, wriggling free until we tumbled to the mats in a tangle of limbs and tears. Should I retreat and observe from afar?

The risk loomed, his unpredictability a shadow over the gathering crowd: the play area attendants, the brothers' father, curious onlookers. Then, an unexpected ally emerged—an older boy, squatting beside us with quiet resolve, his hand steady on the foam stack, a wordless plea for peace. "You shouldn't treat your mum this way," he murmured, his innocence breaking the spell. I touched his arm, whispering through my ache, "He's autistic, but thank you." In that instant, Ilyas glimpsed the wider world, allowing me to reclaim the reins—not with force, but with the fragile thread of connection. Yet his fussing lingered as we departed, the attendant's parting words—"Maybe when it's less busy"—landing like a veiled sting, a reminder of how society so often misreads our struggles.

As we retreated to the car, my mind replayed the chaos: What might have softened the blow? Acknowledging his rage outright—"I see you're angry; it hurts when Mama lets another play with your creation"—could have bridged the gap, but from his distant vantage point at the slide's peak, containment felt impossible. Dismissing his fury with smiles only fuelled it, a misstep born of the moment's heat. Could I have intercepted those wild throws, redirecting his energy? His actions, devoid of malice yet fraught with harm, compelled me to whisk him away, though pleas like "Let's drink water and return" fell on ears drowned in emotion. In the aftermath, seated beside him, I wove a gentle narrative: "Feel the cool water sliding down your tummy? Remember how hot and red your face felt before? Mama knows when you're upset. I'm sorry I let the boy slide—it was fast and fun for him, just like it is for you." This ritual—calming with water, a soothing stroke along his limbs, or a rocking embrace—describes the body's storm, linking physical sensations to the fury's tide. For children as young as four, it plants seeds of mindfulness: observing anger's grip on the eyes, the hands, then releasing it to reclaim joy's warmth.

AM I OBSERVANT?

Such learnings, drawn from books and experts, shimmer with promise—yet they often falter in the raw pulse of crisis, for no script can anticipate the organic chaos of each storm. Neurodivergent anger, layered with unspoken frustrations, defies rote responses; it calls for presence attuned to the moment's unique rhythm. Practice alone hones this art: with each encounter, we refine our instincts, responding not with rigid formulas but with empathetic grace. Over time, like a desert bloom after rare rain, we grow adept at navigating these tempests—transforming outbursts into opportunities for deeper bonds, where understanding blooms and society learns to hold space for every soul's intricate dance.

Beyond managing anger, children and our loved ones on the spectrum experience anxiety. Anxiety is fear of the future, especially when it is uncertain. An autistic individual benefits from having their days and weeks planned; for children, this is accomplished with visual calendars.

Since my son was a young toddler, the calendar was a minimal kind that showed a 2-step instruction: First wake up, then toilet. Or: First wash hands, then eat. This progressed to 3-step timelines: First wake up, then toilet, last breakfast. We are able to add to the steps as they grow older, turning it into a full day's schedule.

My son gets anxious when we go to the hospital because we had forced him to sit, holding his arms against his will so that the phlebotomist draws blood for a genetic test. Ilyas now knows the features that make a hospital a hospital: the laminate floorings, the rails on the walls, the scrubs that nurses and doctors wear. Last time we went to the hospital I had to calm Ilyas down. Deep breathing is scientifically proven to reduce stress by activating the parasympathetic nervous system. Getting Ilyas to take deep breaths was an exercise I learnt from a yoga instructor who gave a children's session at the Abu Dhabi Book Fair. She had all the children sitting in a circle and asked them to take a deep breath, hold, then exhale making different animal noises:

- Make a snake noise, "Sssssss, who can make the longest Ssssss" and stroke a finger up the child's chest to follow the movement of the air as they exhale it.
- Make a fish noise, with the children's mouths rounded in little circles and pursing their lips gently as if popping mouth bubbles so their exhalations trickle slowly out of their chests.
- Make an elephant noise of trumpeting. Mimicking an elephant's trunk, the children would bring their hands close to their chin and move it upwards as they exhale "Ooomph", with their hands gesturing the loud vibrations of the elephant's trumpet.

These breathing exercises are best done daily or frequently as we play with our children in their stable states (no fear or anxiety) to maintain their awareness of the effects of breathing to their bodies. When I am in the hospital with Ilyas, he is already anxious and not in a playful mood, so my trick is to get him to smell lavender essential oil that I keep in a small bottle hanging from a keychain. This helps him re-centre; the scent is calming, inviting Ilyas to take deeper breaths. Once I have him settled, I engage with him with fun activities. (His favourite is getting a piggy-back ride.) With Ilyas on my back I gallop like a horse along the hospital's corridors, and we make a stop at some of the hanging photographs (the history of UAE's sheikhs visiting the hospital) or hanging posters with patient guidelines, where I ask Ilyas to point to a specific number, word, or person in the posters.

Helping children calm down is the first step to managing meltdowns or tantrums, and a critical part of developing a child's emotional resilience that grounds them as they grow into adulthood. The child's model of adulthood is his/her parents, hence we need to set an example of self-regulation. Remember this the next time you are frustrated at your child and about to let your anger go at them untamed. This is your chance to model self-regulation, taking deep breaths, counting, even narrating what you're going through: "Mama is upset because Ilyas is tossing items around"; "Mama is taking a deep breath, closing my eyes, let the air out 'whooo', opening my eyes, and smiling."

"Ilyas do you see Mama? Do you see everything on the floor because you tossed them? Let us clean up." As I start cleaning up, I would approach Ilyas and explain to him that we need to respect items in our own or a friend's house. Lastly, end with "Thank you Ilyas for cleaning up" or "Good job cleaning!"

As parents, we do not need to be perfect. Showing our children that we also go through struggles provides them with the experience and practical tools required to guide their emotions. Instead of focusing on doing things the right way, parents only need to be consistent and present in their children's stressful moments, which will only become bigger and more stressful as they age.

Being observant takes practice and prioritising what's important. While most of us are tired from all the distractions we go through in our days, having a meaningful conversation with a friend, a purposeful interaction with a neighbour, or a playful session with a child will leave you energised and not fatigued. That is because you are in sync with your and your counterpart's emotions. Start today by choosing one situation with your child or loved one to observe mindfully—note environmental cues and body language, then reflect on how it transforms your interaction. This leads us to the practice of sensing, where we delve deeper into understanding sensitivities to empathise with neurodivergent experiences.

5

AM I SENSING?

Tuning into sensitivities for deeper empathy

Have you ever walked into a room and felt overwhelmed by a scent or noise that others barely noticed, wondering if you're "too sensitive"? Such experiences are daily realities for neurodivergent individuals, highlighting how sensing our surroundings can bridge gaps in understanding.

Being sensitive is another practice that will fundamentally change your interactions with people. This chapter focuses on the practice of sensing, a critical trait for parents and caregivers to recognise and empathise with the heightened sensitivities of neurodivergent children like Ilyas. You will learn how sensing helps identify antecedent factors to behaviours and promotes inclusive interactions by understanding unique sensory processing. By the end of this chapter, you will be able to cultivate sensing in your daily life to support neurodivergent individuals, creating environments that honour their experiences and foster belonging in society. You will have the confidence to address a situation when you empathise with a dysregulated individual's emotions, so that the solution you offer benefits the individual.

Understanding Children's Communication Through Sensitivity

As parents, we long to connect with our children, to make them feel heard, understood, and cherished. Yet, too often, we slip into autopilot, distracted by endless tasks, nodding through conversations while our minds wander. This happens not just with our children but in all our relationships. True sensitivity, however, calls us to be fully present, to tune into the subtle ways our children communicate—through cries, gentle tugs, or fleeting glances. By engaging the eight senses—sight, hearing, touch, taste, smell, proprioception, vestibular, and interoception—we can notice when a child is dysregulated, their emotions or senses overwhelmed, and respond with the empathy they need to feel safe.

Being dysregulated in any sense may cause the body to enter survival mode, hence deeming it less likely to understand the current situation or inputs. There are eight senses identified, mentioned below as taken from sensoryhealth.org:

1. Visual: responsible for seeing.
2. Auditory: responsible for hearing.
3. Olfactory System: responsible for processing smell.
4. Gustatory System: responsible for the sense of taste.
5. Tactile System: responsible for processing touch information from the body.
6. Vestibular System: contributes to balance and orientation in space. It is the leading system informing us about movement and position of the head relative to gravity.
7. Proprioceptive System: senses the position, location, orientation, and movement of the body muscles and joints.
8. Interoception: internal sensors that provide a sense of what our internal organs are feeling. Hunger and thirst are examples of interoception.

Understanding our senses for ourselves assists in communicating our needs. When an individual is regulated in all their senses, they are able to communicate their wants. When the individual is not regulated, they may prefer not to communicate until they are satisfied in all their senses; maybe their hearing is impaired due to the sun being too bright, or they are fatigued due to hunger, or they are running on a full bladder and are unable to communicate their need for a toilet break.

Communicating is not limited to words. Beyond verbal and body language, Augmentative and Alternative Communication (AAC) refers to all forms of communication that do not focus on speech because many individuals are verbally challenged due to various conditions, such as developmental disabilities, acquired disorders, or even in temporary situations like recovering from a surgery. Different forms of communication, such as echolalia, written expression, and body language, should be understood and supported.

Sensitivity Beyond Words: The Language of the Senses

Sensitivity means seeing beyond words to the rich language of a child's senses and behaviours. Many assume communication is mostly verbal, but children, especially those who are neurodivergent, often express themselves through non-verbal cues—crying, pointing, or subtle shifts in posture. For instance, my non-verbal son, Ilyas, doesn't say "yes" or "no". For the longest time, I thought he always rejected everything and anything I had to offer since he knew how to shake his head left and right meaning no; otherwise, I hadn't noticed any nods to mean yes.

It wasn't until summer 2024 when I took Ilyas to try therapy in Dubai that the behavioural therapist helped me see Ilyas's "yes": a rare direct look into my eyes was his way of saying "yes". That moment of connection, so easy to miss, taught me to watch closely for his signals. By responding joyfully—"Yes, Ilyas wants this!"—I reinforce his communication, building trust. Sensitivity to the eight senses helps us catch these cues: a clenched fist (touch), a startled flinch at noise (hearing), or a spinning sensation (vestibular), all signs of dysregulation that call for our calm presence.

Empowering Expression Through Neuro-Affirming Sensitivity

Being neuro-affirming means embracing neurological differences as natural, not intentional misbehaviour. Autistic children, for example, may become dysregulated when their sensory world feels chaotic—unable to hear our words, feel the ground beneath them, or process what triggered their distress. Sensitivity allows us to recognise these moments and offer comfort to shift their state from overwhelm to calm. When we validate their feelings—through a gentle touch (touch), a soothing voice (hearing), or simply sitting close—we help them feel seen. Empowering children to express their needs, whether through echolalia, gestures, or pictures, transforms their internal chaos into something tangible they can share. This requires us to observe their sensory cues across all eight senses and respond with patience, helping them navigate their world.

Unveiling the Layers: Understanding Neurodivergent Expressions Through Empathy

In the intricate world of neurodivergence, certain behaviours—often misunderstood or vilified by neurotypical observers—serve as profound windows into an individual's inner turmoil. Headbanging, self-harm, and aggression, far from being mere disruptions, are adaptive responses, cries from a mind navigating overwhelming sensations and emotions. Recently, I had the privilege of speaking with a successful autistic adult, thriving in her career and life, who illuminated these expressions with the clarity of lived experience, urging us toward compassion rather than judgement.

Consider headbanging. This is often misunderstood by neurotypical perspectives as mere disruption, but in truth, it is a vital form of self-regulation and comfort for autistic individuals. It provides a focused, rhythmic pressure that alleviates the overwhelming buildup in their minds—stemming from confusion, stress, or emotions that swirl too intensely to articulate. I've witnessed this firsthand with my own child, whose early expressions of it shattered my heart like fragile glass. In those tender years, amid surges of distress, my little one would instinctively seek that grounding sensation against a surface, a raw attempt to soothe an inner storm. Over time, a quiet adaptation emerged: a small hand placed as a buffer,

AM I SENSING?

a heartbreaking yet hopeful sign of emerging self-awareness and resilience.

The memory of one particularly painful moment lingers, tied to a developmental milestone for personal hygiene we were navigating together. I had noticed the subtle cues signalling a private, vulnerable process, one my child guarded fiercely. Yet, swayed by well-meaning but insistent advice from my own upbringing—that I wasn't guiding "correctly" and must intervene forcefully—I overrode my intuition. In that instant, I stepped in, disrupting the natural flow, only to witness an outpouring of frustration that escalated into self-soothing through headbanging. It was a profound misstep, enveloping us both in a wave of regret and sorrow. As I held my child close, tears blurring my vision, I realised the folly of clinging to rigid, inherited methods that ignored the unique rhythm of growth. From that day, I committed to honouring space—allowing my child to unfold at their own pace, free from imposed timelines or outdated expectations, fostering a bond rooted in trust and gentle understanding. In embracing this, we not only nurture resilience but model an inclusive world where every individual's way of being is respected, not reshaped.

Self-harm, too—manifesting as biting, scratching, or even rejecting food—emerges as a conduit for emotions that defy verbal escape, whether joy, sorrow, excitement, or rage. Praise be to Allah, Ilyas radiates happiness, and I pray to nurture in him a profound gratitude for divine blessings enveloping us all.

Yet, these acts often distil pent-up feelings, releasing them like steam from a pressured valve.

I know self-harm from my own quiet struggles; in my pre-teen years, anger would rise within me like an unexpected storm, leading to petty squabbles with my younger brother over the smallest things. When that inner turmoil built to a breaking point, I'd reach for scissors, opening them to trace a faint line across my skin just above the wrists, finding a fleeting sense of release as the tension ebbed away, like letting go of a tightly held breath. I'd hide the marks under long sleeves and chunky bracelets, the original spark of frustration fading into obliviousness. This fleeting phase didn't last long, even as darker trends like gothic emo styles began to emerge in school during the early 2000s. It came to an abrupt end when my mother noticed my arms one day in the kitchen, as we cleared the lunch table together. Her reaction was swift and firm, rooted in the protective ways of her generation—she reminded me sternly of the sanctity of our bodies as God's gift, urging me to treat my own with care and purpose. In those times, parenting often leaned on direct correction rather than delving into the "why", reflecting an era that prioritised guiding children through authority over fostering their emotional independence to explore and express feelings on their own. Her words, though delivered without deeper inquiry, carried the weight of concern, helping me step away from the habit and toward a path of greater self-respect.

Aggression toward others, meanwhile, often erupts from environmental overload—blaring lights, cacophonous noise, sweltering heat, or chilling cold—elements beyond the individual's control that flood their senses like a relentless storm. With Ilyas, this surfaces when transitions loom, like leaving the pool after play; he'll seek objects to hurl, from hefty trash bins to whatever's at hand—even my phone, or comically, attempting to fling my arms skyward, which I swiftly transform into a triumphant "Hooray!" to redirect his energy and defuse the tension.

These insights underscore why our body language, silent cues, and inner equilibrium are paramount: by staying composed, we mirror calm, guiding our children back to serenity. Yet in a world that barrels forward relentlessly, tranquillity feels elusive. As I sat with Ilyas on that roadside asphalt, fries in hand, I battled worries about our impending doctor's appointment slipping away. Mothers bear endless burdens, so I whisper "Bismillah" before every step, invoking divine alignment with life's twists. I've beheld all three behaviours in my son, and the maternal ache of witnessing such "negative" displays—yearning to intervene yet holding back—is profound. But presence trumps props or platitudes; when our children spiral, our own upset ignites—tensing muscles, racing hearts, primal urges to quell the storm. Here's the overlooked truth: our emotional steadiness outshines any technique. Children anchor to our calm; without it, deep breaths or logic falter.

Corrections unfold later, in peaceful interludes—replaying scenarios through play or stories where characters navigate similar losses, with Ilyas as the empathetic guide. We'll explore these soon. Remember, such tools prepare us, but true readiness blooms from observing and reflecting (as in the next chapter), empowering co-regulation in the moment. Ultimately, regulating our emotions sharpens our gaze, transforming observation from mere vigilance into a profound act of love, fostering an inclusive society where neurodivergent expressions are met not with apprehension and fear, but with understanding and grace.

Overcoming Barriers to Sensitivity: A Personal Reflection

When I was in elementary school I had to study the mathematical multiplication table. The assignment was for digits 1 to 10 and it just looked like long columns of numbers on a black and white page. My dad was teaching me, which was not the usual, since he mostly spent his afternoons napping while my mum took care of our studies. I did not know the meaning of mathematics, nor the meaning of studying. At some point I asked my mum: If the information is in the book and I know where it is, why does it need to be in my head? The concept of studying was foreign to me and it wasn't until later stages in school that I grasped an understanding of education and memorisations. So, I was on the floor with my dad pointing at these numbers on the white page and I couldn't answer him; I probably didn't even know he was expecting the answer to be a number.

My dad became very upset, raising his voice, which caused me to stress. I remember feeling the room spinning (vestibular), losing sense of the carpet under me (touch), and seeing my peripheral vision turn black like black fog was forming in front of my eyes (sight). I was dizzy and my mind drifted off somewhere else, since I couldn't understand the pressure my dad placed on me to answer what 2×2 was. Looking back, I see how my father's lack of sensitivity to my sensory and emotional state deepened my distress. Had he noticed my trembling hands or racing heart (interoception), he might have paused to comfort me. This experience taught me that sensitivity isn't just about noticing—it's about acting with care to restore calm, especially when a child's senses are overwhelmed. Hence, sensitivity plays a role in building trust and strengthening relationships within families and communities.

The Impacts of Not Listening

During one of my jobs in the healthcare industry, I interacted with an Emirati lady who was acting in the role of Chief Human Capital Officer. Whenever I spoke to her, she made me feel like I was the only one in the room, even when her team members were there to check off HR matters. Once she saw me, her eyes locked in to mine with full attention. It felt like there was a bubble enclosing us and whatever I had to say would reach her and she was ready to receive it, acknowledging my presence and my requests. If you have someone like that in your life, cherish and learn from them. I want my child to feel the warmth that engulfed my interactions at work. A warmth that fills his heart when I listen to him, when I engage with him (since he is still non-verbal), and when I grasp the little gestures' meanings. Not just nodding to my son but seeing into his soul. This is what our children crave in every moment they turn to us—to feel valued, to know they matter. When we are present in body but lost in thought, distracted by the endless tasks of life, our children sense it. Their young hearts, so open and tender, pick up on our absence through their senses— the way our eyes wander (sight), the flatness in our voice (hearing), or the tension in our touch (touch). These moments of half-listening teach them not just about our attention but about their own worth in a world full of distractions. Research shows that even children as young as three respond differently when we truly listen. Their words flow more freely, their emotions settle more easily, and their confidence grows when we tune in with all our senses, noticing the subtle cues of their joy or dysregulation.

The Lasting Impact of Authentic Listening

When we listen to our children with our whole being, the effects ripple far beyond that fleeting moment. Studies on early childhood show that children who feel truly heard develop stronger emotional intelligence, learning to name their feelings and trust their voices. This sensitivity to their needs—through the eight senses, like hearing their trembling voice or seeing their furrowed brow—helps them grow into listeners themselves. In the classroom, these children focus better and understand others more deeply. At home, they mirror this care with siblings and friends, perhaps sharing stories under the shade of a tree, as we do in our gatherings. Most beautifully, they carry this gift of connection into adulthood, building relationships rooted in empathy and understanding. By listening with sensitivity today, we shape how our children will listen, love, and connect for a lifetime, even becoming better parents than us.

The Weight of the Mental Load

The weight of parenting is heavy like a basket overflowing with dates, each one a task, worry, or plan that never seems to lighten. It's not just the distractions—it's the endless mental dance of keeping everything together: the schedules, the meals, the unspoken fears of forgetting something vital. Being the one who knows the when, where, and how of every moment—like ensuring the children's school needs are met or the family's Ramadan gatherings are prepared—feels like a role with no pause. This mental load can consume us, pulling our focus away from the sensory cues our children send to signal their dysregulation, like a furrowed brow (sight) or a restless fidget (proprioception). Sensitivity requires a clear mind, but the constant juggling often clouds our ability to truly see and hear our little ones.

As Eid draws near, my heart swells with anticipation, but also a quiet worry. For my son Ilyas, who navigates the world through a sensitive lens, this joyous day brings challenges: wearing a special outfit, sitting in a formal space, and greeting a flurry of unfamiliar faces. The kandoora, our traditional white garment worn for Eid's celebrations, is meant to honour the occasion's sanctity, but its flowy, synthetic fabric prickles against Ilyas's skin (touch), unlike the soft cotton he loves. To ease his discomfort, I layer a cotton t-shirt and light shorts underneath, leaving the tight neckline unbuttoned—a small victory if he keeps it on at all. Some Eids, I let go of the kandoora entirely, content with his comfort. Other years, he'd wear it just long enough for a family photo, shedding it after twenty minutes of fidgeting (proprioception).

But one Eid, my heart leapt when Ilyas saw his father in his kandoora and insisted on wearing his own, mirroring his role model. That moment, a milestone in his sensory journey, felt like a gift brighter than the Eid moon.

On Eid morning, we visit my grandparents' home, the heart of our family's gatherings. The majlis, our formal lounge where women and men gather separately, hums with chatter and laughter (hearing), a vibrant yet overwhelming space for Ilyas. At home, he loves bouncing on a single sofa, but we've gently taught him that jumping isn't for public spaces like malls or clinics. In the majlis, the expectation to offer Salam—shaking hands with a warm "Salamu Alaikum"—is a cherished ritual, one Ilyas knows from daily greetings. Yet, on Eid, the crowd of new faces and voices can flood his senses of hearing and sight, leading to dysregulation. After a few handshakes, he might dart in and out of the door or race up the stairs (which I used to recognise as a distracting activity but is actually engaging vestibular and proprioception senses to seek relief from the sensory storm). When he was younger, this overwhelm would drain him, and he'd curl up for a nap in a guest room downstairs, a quiet haven in my grandparents' welcoming home. As an Emirati mother, I once worried that I couldn't prepare Ilyas for Eid's unique demands, which come only twice a year. But as he's grown, his resilience has blossomed. Now, he can join me in the women's majlis or his father in the men's, staying engaged for half the day—a triumph of his growth and our shared journey in understanding his needs.

The Energy Drain of Parenting

By the time we sit with our children, our hearts long to connect, but our energy is often spent, like a lamp flickering at the end of a long night. The advice to "be present" feels out of reach when we're exhausted from the day's demands—preparing meals, guiding bedtime prayers, or soothing a restless child. Many parents, especially those with little support, forget to nurture themselves. A 2024 Surgeon General report highlighted how parenting can strain mental health, and I see this in my own life, raising my child in a bustling world, and in the tired eyes of other mothers. Some days, it takes all we have to serve a simple meal or tuck our little ones into bed before collapsing. Yet, refilling our own energy—through rest, reflection, or community—allows us to tune into our children's sensory needs, like their trembling voice (hearing) or unsteady movements (vestibular), with the sensitivity they deserve.

As a mother, I know the weight of wanting to be fully present for my children, yet feeling pulled by the demands of life—like preparing for a family iftar or ensuring the home is ready for guests. Sensitivity isn't about having endless energy or perfect focus; it's about using our hearts and senses wisely to connect with our children, especially when their emotions run high. By tuning into their sensory cues—through their eyes (sight), gestures (touch), or trembling voices (hearing)—we can notice when they're dysregulated and offer the calm they need. In my journey, I've learned that less is more: meaningful connection trumps flawless attention. Drawing from my experiences and insights from *Parent Yourself First*, here are practical tools to listen with sensitivity, fostering trust and understanding with our little ones.

1. **Set a Timer for Presence**: In the rush of daily life, only you know how much energy you can give. Be honest with your child: "My heart, I have five minutes to listen fully to your story or play with you. Then, I'll need a moment to rest." Set a timer and focus wholly on them—no distractions, no multitasking. Watch their face light up (sight) as

they feel your presence, their hands moving freely (proprioception) in play. This small act builds trust, showing them you're truly there, like a warm hug at bedtime. With younger children who are unaware of time you can list the number of times you will play with them, or the number of pages you will read in the book. With Ilyas, I would push him on the swing and then announce that we have 10 more swings to do before dinner time. Also, playing outdoors is fun to set the timer with the sunset and walking back home with the sound of the prayer calling for Maghreb.

2. **Notice Their Hands and Eyes**: When your mind wanders, anchor yourself by observing what your child does with their hands (touch, proprioception). Are they shaping clay or clutching a toy? Join them—pick up a crayon or knead dough beside them, sharing their world. Look at their eyes (sight): what captures their gaze? Showing interest in their focus says, "I value what you love." This connection, like roughhousing and blowing raspberries on their tummies, makes them feel seen and cherished, easing any sensory overwhelm.

3. **Honor Your Own Needs First**: Like a cup of Arabic coffee that needs refilling, you can't pour from an empty heart. If you're hungry or tired (interoception), tell your child: "I want to hear your story, but first, I need a moment to eat or rest. Can you wait five minutes?" Offer a warm hug (touch) and return ready to listen. This teaches patience and shows that caring for yourself strengthens your sensitivity to their needs, like noticing their restless fidgeting (proprioception) when they're dysregulated.

4. **Reflect Their Words Back**: Instead of absent nods or murmurs, echo what your child says to show you're listening. If they share, "I played with a new friend today," respond, "You met a new friend? Tell me more, I'm here." This reflection, paired with a gentle tone (hearing), opens a door to deeper conversation, helping them feel heard. It's like repeating a child's excitement over Eid sweets, affirming their joy and calming their sensory storm. With Ilyas being non-verbal, I listen to the noises he makes and echo it into the nearest sounding word. For example, my son repeats "fook, fook" when he is concentrating on a certain way for playing and I repeat it for him as "focus, Bravo Ilyas, let's focus your fingers to move the car upwards on the Hot Wheels slide." This was a difficult one actually and I didn't know what "fook" meant, but it sounded bad. I had to observe Ilyas's environment closely, then found him repeating "fook" with the swimming coach when the coach was asking Ilyas to focus.

5. **Practise Self-Compassion When You Falter**: Some days, despite your best intentions, your mind drifts—perhaps to a phone or a worry—and your child notices. Don't defend or despair. Place a hand on your heart (interoception) and say, "You're right, my love, I'm struggling to focus. I'm sorry." Take a break: "I need a quiet walk to clear my mind, then we'll read together." This honesty teaches children that it's human to struggle and okay to try again. Avoid self-criticism—it clouds your sensitivity, pulling you away from noticing their subtle cues, like a tense posture (touch) or quickened breath (interoception).

6. **Supporting Material**: Use this sensory sensitivities checklist template to track and adapt:

Sensory Type	Trigger	Child's Reaction	Adaptation Strategy
Sound	Example: loud noises	Covering ears	Use ear muffs
Light	Example: bright lights	Squinting	Dim lighting
Touch	Example: textures	Avoidance	Soft materials
Smell	Example: strong scents	Wrinkled nose	Neutral scents
Balance	Example: movement	Dizziness	Stable activities

For a step-by-step example: During therapy at Clinic #2, sense Ilyas's discomfort from air conditioning, adjust the temperature, and note improved focus. Resources: Read "Understanding Neurodiversity Through a Sensory Lens" on sensoryhealth.org or "Sensory Differences – A Guide for All Audiences" on autism.org.uk.

Your child doesn't need perfect presence—just the warmth of knowing you're trying, heart and senses open. Start with one moment of true listening, like sitting close during a bedtime story, and watch the trust grow. Sensitivity transforms these small moments into lasting bonds, like the roots of a tree anchoring a family through time.

Overcoming Barriers: The Vital Simplicity of Sensitivity and its Profound Impact on a Child's Nervous System

In the relentless rhythm of daily life, it's all too easy to drift from the quiet signals our children send, their subtle cues drowned out by the clamour of distractions, bone-deep fatigue, or the weight of unspoken worries. These barriers obscure the sensory whispers that hint at their inner dysregulation, pulling us from the profound attunement we yearn to offer. Yet, embracing sensitivity demands we confront these obstacles not with harsh self-criticism, but with tender honesty and self-compassion— a soothing balm that clears the fog from our hearts, inviting us to engage with grace and full presence. By savouring all eight senses, we forge a deeper bond, one that honours the unique neurodivergent pathways of children like my son, Ilyas, fostering a society where every individual's sensory world is met with empathy and understanding.

At the heart of it all lies the child's brain, a delicate archive of emotions and repeated experiences, where familiar moments etch themselves into the neural wiring that shapes their very essence. Simple backyard play, for instance, emerges as a cornerstone of healthy development: its steady, predictable rhythms, paired with emotional co-regulation and a tapestry of sensory input, nurture growth in ways grand adventures cannot rival. When a child senses safety in the steady gaze of a caring adult, their nervous system unwinds, transforming tension into tranquillity and opening pathways for learning, exploration, and expansion. This magic unfolds not in extravagant outings, but in the ordinary sanctuaries of home—splashing through sprinklers, squelching in mud puddles, or feeling the cool grass under bare feet—all weaving intricate sensory maps that fortify attention, refine movement, and cultivate emotional resilience.

Consider this: a humble AED 1 popsicle can ignite more radiant joy than a lavish AED 100 theme park visit, provided it arrives wrapped in true attunement. It's your face—lit with genuine delight and undivided focus—that renders the memory enchanting, imprinting it on their soul. Children, especially those navigating neurodivergence, thrive not on ceaseless stimulation but on responsive, heartfelt presence. In these slowed-down interludes, where life pauses enough to truly feel, the brain flourishes, its nervous system soothed into a state of receptivity that builds lasting strength. This simplicity is no small gift; it's the critical thread weaving inclusive societies, where sensitivity becomes the bridge to honouring every child's inner world, allowing them to bloom without the shadows of misunderstanding.

I am sensitive when I am able to acknowledge someone else's emotions, tune into their feelings, and help them regulate what they are going through. Many diverse-ability individuals do not know how to express emotions, positive or negative. This may cause an outburst of challenging behaviour. Hence sensing ourselves first to be grounded, then approaching our children or our caretakers with an anchoring calm, steady sight, and gentle touch allows their nervous system to feel safe. Remember that emotions such as anxiety are contagious; they flow from one nervous system to the next in proximity. Sensing is fundamental in empathising with neurodivergent sensitivities, so practise the steps for sensing and learn to prevent misinterpretations. Identify one sensory trigger in your child's routine today and adapt the environment, reflecting on the change in their response.

Now that we have learnt two fundamental daily practices, we need to learn to maintain them and build our agility to face any situation. The third practice that helps your growth is reflection, which we will discuss next in Chapter 6.

6

AM I REFLECTING?

Reflecting is the daily practice that will help you become more observant, sensitive, and regulated

> "Bring yourself to account before you are taken to account (on the Day of Judgement)."
>
> —Omar Bin Al Khattab

In a world that urges constant action, what if pausing to reflect on a single interaction with your child could transform your relationship and society's view of neurodivergence?

This chapter delves into the transformative power of reflection in parenting and beyond. We explore two facets: the introspective review of our lifelong parenting experiences, which uncovers hidden triggers from our past, and the daily habit of mindful pause, which refines our interactions in the present. Through personal stories and timeless wisdom, we'll see how shifting from reactive control to conscious connection fosters empathy—not just for our children, but for ourselves and society at large. By embracing reflection, we build bridges of inclusion, honouring the unique journeys of all individuals, including those who are neurodivergent.

In the quiet aftermath of life's fleeting moments, we often pause to revisit our reactions, only to find them waning. As we recount a story to a friend or replay it silently in our minds, the slower pace of reflection unveils nuances we missed—the sharpness of a word, the subtlety of a gesture, even the fleeting arch of a frown or the warmth of a nod. These insights, born from hindsight, invite us to grow, transforming regret into wisdom.

The Dual Dimensions of Reflection

In this chapter, we explore reflection in two profound dimensions: the broader lens of introspection on our parenting journey, spanning years of accumulated experiences, and the intimate practice of daily review, examining the fresh imprints of recent encounters. Both forms empower us to evolve, fostering deeper connections with our children and ourselves.

Reflective functioning, at its core, is the art of weaving our past into the present—understanding how our history shapes the way we appear in our children's lives. For generations, we've been conditioned to view parenting as a hierarchy: parents as authoritative figures wielding control, children as obedient vessels moulded to fit. But this outdated paradigm must give way to conscious parenting, where true connection flourishes. Raising a child isn't merely about guiding them; it's an invitation to elevate our own consciousness. Through this process, we heighten our self-awareness, unlocking better outcomes for our little ones and healing the unseen wounds within us.

Guiding, Not Governing: Honouring Our Children's Paths

Our children embark on journeys uniquely their own—we are not the architects of their paths but gentle guides, redirecting their vibrant energies along trails they intuitively carve. Too often, we impose maps drawn from our own unresolved childhoods, stifling their natural exploration. Mistakes are inevitable milestones on their way; as parents, our role is to accompany them through the stumbles, not to clear every obstacle or instil a fear of failure. A rigid upbringing, where errors are erased or harshly punished, traps children in an illusion of perfection, hindering their emotional and mental growth. As they venture beyond the family nest, they may grapple with addictions, depression, or unhealthy relationships—echoes of unaddressed inner turmoil. To shepherd them with grace, we must first forge unbreakable bonds of love and connection, the bedrock of any enduring parent–child relationship.

Connect Before Correct: A Universal Principle

The wisdom of 'connect before correct' resonates deeply in our Islamic heritage, as embodied by the Prophet Muhammad (peace be upon him), who outlined children's development in three nurturing stages. This principle was echoed in a professional training I attended on mindsets, illustrated by the Arbinger Institute's pyramid—a framework for human interactions that prioritises relationships over immediate fixes. In that moment, I turned to my colleagues and shared, "This isn't just for the workplace; it's a blueprint for parenting." Indeed, the essence of connecting with others—whether as a mother soothing her son, a colleague collaborating on a project, or a driver navigating traffic with quiet patience—mirrors the heart of parenting itself.

Traditional parenting often relies on rote tools: scripted phrases for every mishap, reward charts to motivate, or threats of punishment to deter. But what if we turned inward first, tending to our own mental and emotional wellbeing to create a calmer space for our children? True attunement begins with self-examination, acknowledging how our histories colour our responses.

Echoes of the Past: When History Intrudes on the Present

How often do we, in a moment of exasperation, gently scold a child who turns away from their meal by reminding them of those less fortunate, far away, who hunger for even a morsel? Or, when their restlessness tests our patience, softly echo tales of our own childhoods, where simple tasks filled our days without the luxuries they know? I remember my own tender vulnerability during my son's gradual journey through a key milestone, the repeated efforts leaving me weary, until one quiet afternoon, my voice rose unexpectedly: "At your age, I was already helping with chores around the house." Those words, slipping out in fatigue, gave me pause—a gentle nudge from my past, whispering that unresolved echoes can sometimes colour our present with our children.

Reflective parenting invites us to awaken to these patterns, choosing consciousness over autopilot. Our childhood memories bubble up not as burdens, but as beacons—illuminating how our parents' limitations, perhaps in dismissing emotions or rushing through life's spiritual depths, left gaps we now have the chance to fill. In these sacred spaces with our children, we heal ourselves too, turning potential conflicts into opportunities for mutual growth. No prenatal class or expert manual can fully prepare us; parenting defies formulas, unfolding organically alongside our child—and the inner child within us, stirred anew by every interaction. It's a dance of trial and error, laced with apologies and insights, where reflection becomes our greatest ally. Each time we pause to reconsider, our minds subtly rewire, paving the way for instinctive grace.

The Power of Positive Language: Reframing Guidance

Consider, for instance, the simple power of positive language with young children, who often latch onto the vivid imagery of words rather than negation. Instead of commanding, "Stop jumping!"—which spotlights the very action we wish to halt—try, "Let's sit quietly on the sofa." The shift is subtle yet profound, guiding behaviour toward calm without resistance. In my own home, I've caught myself defaulting to the negative, only to correct mid-sentence, a small victory born of practice. To embed this habit, rehearse alone: while driving or drifting to sleep, revisit past scenarios and craft affirming alternatives. Speak them aloud, letting the words reshape your instincts, one reflective moment at a time.

Negative	Positive
Stop jumping	Let's sit nicely on the sofa
Don't kick	Use hands to move the chair
No tossing (toys)	Clean up song! Clean up, clean up, everybody everywhere! Clean up, clean up, everybody do your share.
Remove hands (from inside his pants)	Hands up please! Give me a high five—you need clean hands for a high five, so hands outside pants!

Pausing to Respond: Cultivating Empathy in the Moment

In the whirlwind of a challenging moment, the true power of reflection lies in the pause—a deliberate breath before reaction, allowing wisdom to temper instinct. I recall a visit to a friend's home, where my son's innocent curiosity turned into a tense encounter. Enthralled by their pet dog, a creature he knew only from the whimsical cartoons on television, he reached out with unbridled enthusiasm, grasping its fur in a tight, unyielding pull. My heart raced with embarrassment, especially under the gaze of friends, but I forced myself to halt, gathering my composure for both our sakes. Gently, I slipped one hand beneath his to loosen his grip, while the other tickled him lightly, coaxing his fingers to release without harm. All the while, I murmured softly, "Shhh, gentle, gentle," demonstrating with tender strokes on the dog's coat and then on his own arm and back, so he could feel the essence of kindness in action.

In my earlier days, before embracing conscious parenting, my response might have been swift and severe—scooping him up and away, followed by a stern scowl, sparing harsh words in front of others but conveying fear nonetheless. Such knee-jerk reactions often stem from societal pressures that cast neurodivergent individuals—or anyone with diverse abilities—in a negative light, blaming the person rather than the behaviour. Consider a common mishap: a plate of food slips from unsteady hands, shattering on the floor. Instinctively, we might yank the individual aside and scold them, amplifying their sense of failure. Yet reflection opens doors to kinder paths, transforming mishaps into teachable moments:

1. **Clean Up Together**: Grab a wipe or broom and guide them through the process, explaining that messes are widespread but avoidable. Teach that spilled food is no longer safe to eat, emphasising the value of a firm grip. If shards scatter, highlight their sharpness as a gentle warning. Work side by side, directing their hands with care, and end with gratitude: 'Thank you for helping—that's the right way.'
2. **Redirect and Demonstrate**: Shift to a clean space nearby, fetch a fresh plate, and model stability—placing it securely on the table to bear its weight, reducing the risk of another drop. Show how a spoon might nudge it slightly, and teach using the free hand for support, building confidence through practice.

3. **Acknowledge and Apologise**: Offer sincere apologies to those affected, while recognising the onlookers' understanding, fostering a circle of empathy rather than isolation.

These alternatives, rooted in patience and inclusion, seldom emerge in the heat of the moment; our default is often the harshest path, wired by societal patterns that demand conformity. We feel bound by invisible obligations—to appear flawless, to enforce norms—that breed shame when unmet. But when we release these expectations from our bonds with our children, viewing ourselves and them as whole beings, we unravel the cultural threads that label parts of us "good" or "bad". This liberation reveals children as inherently worthy of respect, not as earners of our approval. My love, respect, and connection with my son are unconditional; nothing he does can erode them, for I nurture these qualities in myself first, pouring them outward like a boundless well.

In other trying scenarios, where a positive alternative isn't immediately clear, reflection teaches us to validate emotions before setting boundaries. A child craving chocolate before dinner might hear, "I know you're excited for that treat—it's yummy, isn't it? But can we wait until after dinner?" Mirror their disappointment: "I see you're sad, and that makes me sad too, but dinner will be delicious!" This empathy, delivered with patience, honours their feelings while guiding gently.

The same holds for a beloved iPad, its battery drained: "You're eager to play, and I get that—it's fun! Can you wait while it charges?" Introduce a visual timer, like an hourglass, inviting them to watch the sand trickle (perhaps for five minutes), then flip it once more. These small rituals build anticipation and self-regulation, turning frustration into shared understanding.

For my non-verbal son, these moments become opportunities for growth. I seize them to prompt communication, encouraging a clear request like "I want chocolate, please" or "iPad, please." When he summons the words, even imperfectly, the reward follows swiftly—a celebration of his voice, reinforcing our unbreakable bond in a world that too often silences the neurodivergent. Through reflection, these interactions evolve from mere corrections into profound affirmations of love, paving the way for a more inclusive society where every individual's journey is honoured

The Shadows of Guilt: A Mother's Silent Battle

In the labyrinth of parenthood, guilt lurks like a relentless shadow, whispering accusations of inadequacy at every turn. It's the gnawing belief that we've faltered—that our choices have somehow harmed the very souls we cherish most. Guilt whispers, "You did something wrong," while its darker twin, shame, sneers, "You *are* wrong." This shame breeds fear and anxiety, awakening the wounded inner child within us, crying out for recognition, for attunement. As parents, especially those navigating the uncharted waters of raising a neurodivergent child, we must confront this storm head on. Only by owning our struggles—embracing them not as failures but as catalysts for growth—can we shatter the chains of guilt and step into empowerment, forging paths to solutions that honour both our children and ourselves.

The Weight of "Not Enough": Facing Financial Heartbreak

The storm hit me hardest when I discovered that behavioural therapy—the lifeline my son Ilyas so desperately needed for his autism—was beyond our grasp. My health insurance, a safety net I'd always taken for granted, refused to cover it. The numbers haunted me: an intensive 12 hours a week would demand AED 21,000 monthly, a fortune that slipped through my fingers like desert sand. I settled for six hours, scraping together what I could, but the compromise felt like a betrayal. As an Emirati woman raised in the embrace of the UAE's generosity—where education, healthcare, and even everyday comforts flowed freely—this was my shattering awakening. For the first time, I couldn't summon the resources my child required in my own homeland, a land that had always cradled its citizens in abundance. The guilt crashed over me like a tidal wave: Was I failing as a mother? Had my complacency in this privileged life left me unprepared to fight for my son?

In those dark nights, shame twisted the knife deeper. I envisioned Ilyas's future dimmed by my limitations, his potential stifled because I couldn't bridge this gap. But guilt, if left unchecked, paralyses; it chains us to regret rather than propelling us forward. I refused to let it define me. Instead, I owned the struggle—acknowledging the pain without letting it consume me—and transformed it into fuel. Drawing from the resilient spirit of my ancestors, whose outward-pointing feet navigated treacherous dunes without sinking, I reminded myself: The UAE hadn't just sheltered me; it had equipped me to stand tall, to multiply its gifts through my own strength. Educated and empowered, I was meant to teach, to shelter others, to drift through life's challenges with unyielding confidence. This was my moment to step up.

Unravelling the System: A Quest for Truth and Alternatives

Empowerment began with reflection—a deliberate pause to investigate, to question the barriers before me. For four gruelling weeks, I plunged into a whirlwind of discovery, visiting clinic after clinic, mostly private ones, as public options lagged with endless waitlists and lacked the ABA therapy Ilyas needed. I shuttled him to four hospitals: one for evaluations that peeled back layers of his world, another for psychological insights that pierced my heart, a third for glimpses of ABA's promise, and our familiar haven for ongoing speech and occupational therapy. Each visit was a battlefield—I scrutinised setups, techniques, Ilyas's flickering reactions, the exhausting commutes, and, always, the crushing costs.

Frustration mounted as I challenged my insurance provider: Why fund speech and occupational therapy—already surpassing AED 30,000 in five months—yet deny ABA, which mirrored those expenses but promised deeper transformation? No answers came, only echoes of bureaucracy. Through self-study—an online ABA course—and over a year immersed in rehabilitation's clinical maze, I unearthed a bitter truth: Behavioural therapy had become a commodity, ripe for commercialisation. While speech and occupational therapists endured rigorous medical training, a Registered Behavior Technician (RBT) needed only ABA certification, an exam, and supervised hours—often under a Board Certified Behavior Analyst (BCBA) or Qualified Applied Behavior Analysis (QABA) credentialed overseer. This low barrier invited exploitation: A savvy BCBA could train a team in months, launch a clinic, and peddle packages from 12 to 40 hours weekly, luring desperate parents with cashflow dreams. We paid for one-on-one sessions, then extra for "supervision" that was merely licensing upkeep, inflating bills while our children's needs hung in the balance.

The guilt of navigating this predatory landscape threatened to drown me—had I been naive, trusting a system that profited from vulnerability? But owning the struggle meant reclaiming agency. I refused to be a victim; instead, I enrolled in an Applied Behaviour Analysis Technician (ABAT) course in January 2023, syncing it with Ilyas's nascent home therapy. Weekly online sessions with a seasoned psychologist and fellow parents turned theory into lifeline discussions, bridging the gap between knowledge and action. Yet theory alone wasn't enough—I craved practice, even as a full-time employee juggling endless demands.

Embracing the Chaos: Turning Outings into Lessons of Love

Weekends became my sacred arena, dedicated to Ilyas amid play areas, theme parks, malls, souks, conferences, and exhibitions. In his early days, before therapy's grip, he rebelled against confinement—home was for sleep and sustenance alone. He'd station himself by the door, a silent plea to escape into the world. Outdoors reigned supreme; a simple bench beneath a tree ignited pure joy as he bounded up and down. His autistic rhythms—repetitive paths tapped and retraced, toys rolled in endless loops—were his language, one I learned to honour.

Grocery runs at supermarkets were nightmares: mere minutes in, Ilyas's frustration erupted—kicking shelves, flinging himself from the stroller. The guilt stabbed: was I forcing him into a world that overwhelmed him? Owning this, I pivoted boldly—no more sterile malls. We ventured to the souk, our neighbourhood market, a 40-minute stroll or quick drive away. First, the bakery's warm aroma beckoned; I'd arm Ilyas with coins to "pay" for bread, his excitement palpable as he exchanged them for his gluten treat (before our dietary shift). We'd snag extra pastries for market workers, weaving kindness into our routine.

Next, the fruit vendor: "Point to the apples, habibi!" Bags brimmed with vibrant produce, and I'd teach gratitude as the shopkeeper helped load our car. Laundry pickups followed, with detours to a construction site where Ilyas handed pastries to labourers—his gaze lingering on their hands and clothes, a quiet testament to his growing awareness. The roastery enchanted us last: spices and coffee scents enveloped us like a hug. Ilyas dove into barrels of pulses, his sensory delight once spilling into joyful tosses—now gently curbed, but always met with the owners' warm smiles.

The souk's organic rhythm—free from supermarkets' harsh lights, chemical haze, and artificial chill—nurtured us both. Guilt faded as I saw Ilyas thrive, his meltdowns easing with age. By owning our struggles, we discovered joy in authenticity, proving solutions bloom when we listen to our children's unspoken needs.

From Theory to Triumph: Empowering Through Knowledge

Throughout 2023, we were immersed in behavioural therapy's rhythms—learning, applying, adapting. My ABAT training wasn't just credentials; it was armour, sharpening my interactions with Ilyas, therapists, and doctors. With him, I decoded challenging behaviours, breaking life skills into digestible steps. With therapists, I fuelled progress by spotlighting his loves—outdoor adventures, boundless curiosity. With doctors,

I challenged diagnoses, demanded evidence, and advocated fiercely for tailored paths.

Yet true empowerment demanded self-reflection: parents must see, hear, and understand themselves first. Carving time for solitude, I sat with my truths—accepting, admiring strengths and scars alike. In candid talks with my husband, we unpacked our flaws. His smoking, confined to the bathroom's fan-whirring secrecy, became a flashpoint. "You can't hide this forever," I urged. "Ilyas is sharp; he'll uncover it, and secrets breed lies." I didn't demand he quit—only that he own it openly, admitting human frailty. "We make mistakes," I said. "Admitting them teaches resilience."

Guilt, I realised, was my inner child's echo—yearning for the attunement I craved. By owning it, parents transcend: We model vulnerability, turning struggles into stepping stones. In this ownership lies freedom—not just for us, but for an inclusive society where neurodivergent voices like Ilyas's are celebrated, not shamed.

Breaking the Cycle of Parental Guilt

In the intricate tapestry of parenthood, guilt weaves itself as an uninvited thread, heavy and persistent. It descends upon us in quiet moments—when we overlook a child's whispered tale, our thoughts adrift, or fail to attune to their sensory storms, like the clamour of a bustling room or the scratch of ill-fitting clothes. This guilt spirals into a vicious cycle: the sting of self-reproach pulls us further from presence, amplifying our remorse. Often, it springs from impossible ideals we impose on ourselves—unwavering focus, boundless vigour—while our spirits are already frayed. These unattainable standards, akin to striving for flawlessness amid Eid's whirlwind of traditions and gatherings, only eclipse our inner radiance.

To shatter this cycle, we must cultivate realistic horizons and self-kindness: place a gentle hand over your heart, feel its steady rhythm (a practice of interoception), and affirm softly, "I am giving my all, and that is sufficient." In releasing guilt's grip, we liberate our capacity for empathetic listening, perceiving our children's needs with clarity and fostering unbreakable trust. Just as we nurture our families, we extend this grace outward, our branches offering shade to a community that thrives in inclusivity, embracing all—neurodivergent and beyond.

Nurturing the Child Before You: Beyond Expectations

Conscious parenting demands a profound shift: engaging with the child as they truly are, unbound by our projections or society's rigid moulds. It's not about moulding them to fit an imagined ideal, but honouring their unique developmental rhythms, capacities, and strengths. As the guiding adult, our sacred duty is to foster their growth with compassion. Consider a teenager wrestling with impulse control—we cannot dismiss it with a curt, "You're old enough to know better!" Instead, we pause to witness their inner turmoil and ponder: how can I support wiser choices? This is the essence of psychological scaffolding—offering tools for self-navigation without judgement, building resilience in a world that often overlooks the neurodivergent's nuanced journey.

Tuning into Triggers: The Body's Silent Alarm

Heed your body's whispers in the heat of reaction; they are harbingers of deeper unrest. Anger might coil in your gut, your voice tightens as your throat constricts, your head shakes in denial, or your gaze drifts aimlessly. In reflection's sanctuary—a quiet corner, alone with your thoughts—revisit these flares. Envision yourself in the throes of fury: step through the scenario deliberately, unravelling each thread. Why did your child's action ignite such fire? What unresolved echo from your past amplified the blaze? Triggers, as Bryana of The Conscious Mommy so poignantly describes, arise when "a current situation stirs up unprocessed pain, unmet needs, or unresolved emotions from your own childhood. And while your child might be the spark, the fire is coming from somewhere else." The challenge lies in discernment: Amid the flood of nerves, how do we separate genuine guidance from our own healing cues? This inner conflict, if unaddressed, frays the family's fabric—eroding safety, trust, and authentic bonds. Conscious parents often feel ensnared not by inadequacy, but by inherited patterns lacking compassionate release. Breaking free demands holding these emotions tenderly, healing through relational grace.

From Self-Understanding to Child Empathy: A Mirror of Compassion

Once you've illuminated your own depths, turn that light toward your child: "Now that you see yourself, see your child." If they falter in grasping an instruction—despite your repeated pleas—recognise it's not defiance, but a neural pathway yet unformed. Cease the insistence; draw a deep breath, and pivot to a fresh path. This empathy blooms from self-awareness, transforming frustration into collaborative discovery, especially vital for neurodivergent children whose worlds unfold at their own sacred pace.

Daily Reflection: The Path to Instinctive Grace

Cultivate reflection as a daily ritual—mindful pauses amid the chaos. Change doesn't dawn overnight; grant yourself patience, for one unforeseen day, you'll notice your words flowing with poise, your mind serene, untouched by former storms. In probing a child's behaviour, uphold neutrality: shun labels like "manipulative" or "defiant," which stem from buried biases and societal scripts ingrained since our youth. Approach the raw essence of the action, free from preconceptions, fostering an environment where understanding—and inclusion—can truly flourish.

Mastering Reflection: A Gentle Path to Empathy and Growth

Oh, how I've come to cherish reflection as a quiet anchor in the whirlwind of motherhood, especially with my precious Ilyas, whose autistic world unfolds in ways that demand my deepest attunement. Yet let's be honest—reflection isn't an effortless whisper; it's a deliberate art, one that calls for unwavering focus, the careful unscrambling of events stripped bare of our emotional veils, and a tender exploration of our own hearts amid the chaos. It invites us to linger on those fleeting details—a subtle furrow in Ilyas's brow, a momentary spark in his eyes—that slip away in the heat of the moment, only to reveal profound truths later. This practice deserves its sacred space: perhaps in the hush of bedtime, as the day's echoes fade, or after dinner with a journal in hand, where pen meets paper to chronicle not just the struggles but the subtle triumphs, allowing us to trace our shared journey toward understanding. In nurturing this habit, we don't merely look back; we build bridges of empathy, fostering a society where neurodivergent souls like my son's are embraced with grace, their unique rhythms honoured as vital threads in our collective tapestry.

At its essence, reflection is a purposeful pause—a mindful revisit of our actions and their ripples—to harvest wisdom, particularly in our connections with neurodivergent loved ones, where it cultivates profound empathy and invites adaptive shifts. It's an inner dialogue that challenges our preconceptions, affirming what resonates true while gently dismantling what doesn't, all in service of a more inclusive world. To weave this into your life, as I have in mine, embrace these three guiding steps, each a compassionate invitation to grow:

Step 1: Pause in the Afterglow of Moments.
Right after an encounter—be it a therapy session that left echoes of frustration or a playful interlude tinged with joy—carve out a breath to jot down the essence: what unfolded, the stirrings in your heart, and the subtle cues from your child. For me, this has been transformative, capturing Ilyas's unspoken responses before they dissolve into the day's haze.

Step 2: Uncover the Hidden Patterns and Whys.
Dive into your notes with curiosity, seeking the recurring threads and underlying drives—like Ilyas's acute sensitivity during bowel movements, which I linked to his broader emotional tides. This step isn't about judgement; it's a loving inquiry that reveals the invisible currents shaping behaviours, illuminating paths to deeper connection.

Step 3: Weave Insights into Gentle Change.
Armed with these revelations, refine your approach with kindness—perhaps by allowing a storm of emotions to pass

unchecked, ensuring your responses bloom from patience rather than haste. In this way, reflection becomes a living bridge, not just healing our bonds but inspiring a society where every neurodivergent individual thrives, seen and supported in their fullest light.

- **Supporting material:** Create a reflection journal template.

Date	Interaction Description	My Feelings	Child's Cues	Insights Gained	Next Steps
Example: After home ABA at Clinic #2, reflect on Ilyas's whining, realising its fullness, and plan to offer food later. Resources: "The Value of Special Time and Reflective Listening" on washingtonparent.com or "Positively Parenting your Neurodivergent Child" on positive-education.co.uk					

Soaring Toward Hope: A Flight of Reflection

As the engines hummed to life and our plane lifted into the boundless sky over Abu Dhabi, I gazed out the window, the desert sands blurring into a golden haze below. We were bound for Belgrade, Serbia, in March 2025—a pilgrimage of sorts, chasing the promise of stem cell treatment for my beloved Ilyas. The journey began before dawn, our careful plan a testament to the delicate dance of parenting an autistic child. I'd intended to rouse him at 4 a.m., syncing his rhythms to the flight's demands, but my heart rebelled against stealing his slumber. Instead, I whispered him awake at 5:02, just ahead of his natural 5:10 stirring. The goal? To weave hunger and fatigue into a gentle lull, coaxing him to sleep mid-air after a warm snack. Yet, life's unpredictability wove its own thread: Boarding via bus, a usual trigger for Ilyas's unease, dissolved in the allure of fresh French fries pilfered from his father's croque monsieur. He munched contentedly, eyes wide at the plane's silhouette against the horizon. "That's our airplane," I murmured into his ear, "taking us high into the sky." His tiny protest at the stairs faded as we hurried aboard, the aisle of seated passengers a silent cue: Here, we settle; here, we find our peace.

Turbulence and Tenderness: Navigating the Unknown

The runway stretched like a promise unkept, delaying take-off as I offered Ilyas a lollipop—a premature bribe now spent. No matter; he sipped water to chase the sweetness, his small frame nestling into calm. Then came the roar—the plane surging forward, Ilyas's eyes widening in fear at the velocity, the jolt of turbulence suspending our hearts in ether. Oh, how I prayed he'd one day embrace that thrill, transforming terror into exhilaration! He drifted to sleep on his father's lap, and we eased him between us, a cocoon of love amid the clouds.

In that suspended realm, time folded upon itself. We scrolled through old videos—grainy treasures of Ilyas as a babe, his laughter unshadowed by autism's veil. "Look at him then," I whispered, half-joking, "maybe we shouldn't seek this treatment after all." The words hung heavy, stirring the depths of my soul. We've weathered storms—meltdowns like tempests, silences vast as oceans—yet autism isn't our enemy; it's part of his essence, woven into the boy we adore. Am I altering his core with this intervention? Is it truly "treatment," or a veil lifted to reveal his truest self? Reflection crashed over me like the turbulence below: the uncertainty of ASD clouds every path, demanding we question not just the journey, but the very map we hold. In these quiet altitudes, away from earth's clamour, I pondered our shared odyssey—how embracing his world has reshaped mine, urging society toward inclusion, where neurodivergence isn't a flaw but a facet of humanity's rich tapestry.

Verses of Solace: Finding Light in Sacred Words

As Ilyas slumbered, his breath a rhythmic anchor, I stroked his soft curls, my fingers tracing the innocence of his dreams. Reflection turned inward in this airborne sanctuary, seeking divine guidance. I recited Surah Al-Fatiha, the Quran's opener, each verse a balm for my weary spirit, every word resonating with profound depth amid our quest for healing.

"In the Name of Allah, the Most Beneficent, the Most Merciful"—An invocation of grace, reminding me that mercy envelops even our deepest fears, guiding this mother's heart through uncharted skies.

"All the praises and thanks be to Allah, the Lord of the 'Alamin"—Gratitude swelled within, for the worlds seen and unseen, for Ilyas's light in our lives, urging me to praise amid uncertainty that I am truly grateful for autism.

"The Most Beneficent, the Most Merciful"—His compassion echoed my own hopes, a promise that kindness prevails, even in treatments born of science and faith. God has shown me His mercy and forgiveness so I can be merciful and forgiving in raising my son.

"The Only Owner of the Day of Recompense"—A humbling reminder of ultimate judgement, freeing me from the weight of "what ifs," trusting in a higher plan.

"You Alone we worship, and You Alone we ask for help"—In this plea, I surrendered my burdens, seeking aid not just for Ilyas's body, but for our souls' harmony with God.

"Guide us to the Straight Way"—This verse pierced me, a prayer for clarity in autism's maze, leading us toward inclusion and understanding. On this journey to Serbia, I ask Allah that he blesses this path we are taking.

"The Way of those on whom You have bestowed Your Grace, not of those who earned Your Anger, nor of those who went astray"—A final beacon, illuminating paths of grace over error, inspiring reflection on our choices, fostering a society where every child, neurodivergent or not, walks in light.

In those sacred utterances, reflection crystallised. This flight wasn't mere travel, but a metaphor for our lives, turbulent yet transcendent, where embracing uncertainty births profound growth. As Belgrade drew near, I emerged renewed, ready to advocate for an inclusive world, one reflective step at a time.

Dispelling the Myth: Conscious Parenting as a Pillar of Strength

Ah, the age-old critique that shadows conscious parenting like a persistent cloud: Isn't it just permissive indulgence, a soft surrender to chaos? As a mother raising my autistic son, Ilyas, I've faced this scepticism head-on—from well-meaning relatives who equate firmness with raised voices, to societal whispers that paint empathy as weakness. But let me assure you, dear reader, conscious parenting is neither lax nor feeble; it's a fortress of intentional love, built on the unshakeable belief that true guidance blooms from understanding, not dominance.

In a world quick to label and limit—especially for neurodivergent children like mine—this approach isn't a retreat; it's a revolutionary stand for inclusion, where every child's inherent worth is honoured, fostering a society that celebrates diversity rather than demanding conformity.

At its heart, conscious parenting rejects the notion of children as adversaries to be conquered. Instead, we recognise them as inherently good—pure souls entering the world with open hearts, unmarred by malice or deceit. Ilyas, with his radiant curiosity and unspoken wisdom, reminds me daily: Children aren't born "uncivilised" rebels; they simply arrive without the scripts of societal norms, their behaviours raw expressions of unmet needs or unexplored emotions. A meltdown in the supermarket isn't defiance; it's a cry for attunement, perhaps to overwhelming lights or textures that neurotypical eyes overlook. To dismiss this as naughtiness is to miss the profound opportunity for connection. We, as parents, hold the mirror: If a child lashes out or withdraws, it's often a reflection of our own unresolved shadows—our impatience, our unhealed wounds—that teach them incivility through example. When we fail to accept ourselves, embracing our flaws with grace, we unwittingly pass on that self-rejection, modelling a world where vulnerability is vice and control is king.

Yet, conscious parenting doesn't shy from boundaries; it sets them with unwavering clarity, wrapped in unconditional love. We address unconscious behaviours—not with punishment that breeds shame, but with compassionate redirection that preserves dignity.

Picture this: During one of Ilyas's intense sensory episodes, where the hum of a crowded room triggered his frantic pacing and echolalic echoes, my instinct once screamed to hush him, to conform him to the stares around us. But reflection taught me strength. I knelt to his level, my voice a steady anchor, "I see you're overwhelmed, habibi—let's find a quiet corner together." Boundaries emerged not as walls, but as safe harbours: No harm to self or others, yet space to feel and express. In loving him through the storm—validating his experience while guiding toward calm—I modelled resilience, not rigidity. This isn't permissiveness; it's empowerment, teaching him (and society) that emotions are valid, but choices can be mindful.

Critics may call it weak, but consider the alternative: A punitive path that silences the neurodivergent, enforcing "civility" at the cost of authenticity, breeding resentment and exclusion. Conscious parenting, by contrast, cultivates true strength—inner harmony that ripples outward. When parents accept themselves, flaws and all, we gift our children the freedom to do the same, breaking cycles of judgement. Ilyas's journey has shown me: in this inclusive embrace, society transforms—from a rigid mould into a vibrant mosaic, where every individual, autistic or otherwise, thrives not despite their differences, but because of them. So, let us reflect: true power lies not in control, but in connection—a legacy of love that endures.

Reflecting on our actions, even reflecting on our days' course is a habit and task encouraged by many religions. It seems simple, yet its effects rippled through our developing personalities and disciplined selves. Practising reflection may start with a prayer or at the end of the day alone in bed, looking back at a day's events, recalling actions, words, tone of voice, and facial expressions. Remembering how you felt in a certain moment. While reflecting, you may ask yourself why this happened; with good observation skills, you may have subconsciously picked on a surrounding cue, such as a high temperature, the loud whirring of a fan, or someone picking on your kid without anyone noticing. As you reflect, you may be able to identify your emotions during such incidents, and with practice, you may reach reflective functioning where you can deeply reflect on these emotions from your past.

Try to remember an incident and reimagine it in your head, bringing back all the aspects of the time, place, people, colours, and noises. Then walk through the events in a sequence as if you were narrating a story. Notice your memory strength, and then relax to let your emotions come back. While you are relaxed, ask yourself: what is it that you felt and why?

This chapter on reflecting allows the individual to practise daily and progress their character so that they are able to confidently pursue raising inclusive societies as they embark on reaching out to community services such as schooling for children, healthcare for diverse-abilities family members, or employability for people of determination.

SECTION 3

PROGRESSING

In this culminating section, we turn our focus outward, examining the profound responsibilities each of us bears toward our communities and the broader society. Whether you are a devoted parent, a dedicated educator, or someone balancing the demands of professional life with the nurturing of your family, the personal practices explored in Section 2—observing, sensing, and reflecting—must transcend the intimate sphere of home. They call us to extend our empathy and awareness into the larger ecosystem, where individual growth intersects with collective progress. Here, we delve into society's pivotal role in amplifying these habits, transforming solitary introspection into shared action. As we hone our ability to observe nuances, sense unspoken needs, and reflect on our interactions, we naturally deepen our engagement—with neighbours, communities, and the world at large. Thus, this section illuminates the community's essential function in fostering inclusive environments that uplift every child, particularly those with neurodivergence or diverse abilities. We begin with Chapter 7, "Are We Accepting?," followed by "Are We Advocating?," and conclude with "Are We Inclusive?," charting a path from personal awakening to societal harmony, where families like mine, raising children like Ilyas, find not isolation but a welcoming embrace that honours all.

7

ARE WE ACCEPTING?

Acceptance goes beyond knowing the meaning; it is empathy for the lived experiences of people of determination

"Diagnosed but mum said no." In a world that idolises "normal," what if the *truly* strange thing is expecting everyone to fit the same mould, ignoring the rich tapestry of neurodivergent experiences?

This chapter offers a thoughtful critique of the notion of "normal" through the lens of neurodivergence, drawing upon my personal encounters with Ilyas to reveal how entrenched societal expectations often hinder rather than empower those who diverge from them. You will be guided to interrogate these norms and champion a more expansive worldview that honours individuality. By the chapter's close, you will possess the tools to identify and dismantle biases rooted in "normalcy," thereby advancing an inclusive society that cherishes every ability as a vital contribution. Through the narrative of my own awakening to autism—including the poignant delays in seeking diagnosis—you will come to grasp the profound repercussions of denial and partial acceptance: from the isolation bred by a community's unawareness, spanning therapists, educators, and even kin, to the fragmented support Ilyas received across various institutions, and the well-intentioned yet inadequate responses from family that ultimately fell short of true solidarity.

Whispers of Concern: The Gentle Dawn of Discovery

In the shadowed corridors of early motherhood, where love and uncertainty intertwined like vines in a desert oasis, the first whispers of concern for my son Ilyas emerged not as a thunderclap, but as a gentle, insistent breeze. He was just one year and eight months old when we embarked on speech therapy—a light-hearted addition to his budding routine, twice-weekly sessions that slipped seamlessly into our lives like a cherished ritual. The centre nestled near our apartment, a short jaunt that either his father or I savoured, cradling him in our arms as we stepped into those forty-five minutes of guided exploration.

ARE WE ACCEPTING?

It began innocently enough, prompted by my mother's well-meaning observation: Ilyas, bathed in the melodies of three languages at home—Arabic's rhythmic warmth, English's ubiquitous flow, and French's elegant cadence—might simply need a nudge to find his voice amid the linguistic tapestry.

English enveloped us like a familiar cloak, the lingua franca of our daily world: greetings in elevators, chatter with the nanny, the hum of shopping excursions. At home, it bridged the gap between my husband's native French and my own Arabic roots; we understood snippets of each other's tongues, yet never fully immersed ourselves in mastery, content in our shared fluency. French danced through Ilyas's ears in his father's firm yet loving commands, which he obeyed with startling precision, or in the whimsical tunes of nursery rhymes and Peppa Pig episodes that lit up his face with delight. Arabic, my heart's first song, wove in during visits to my family, phone calls with my mother, or the soul-stirring strains of music during our car rides. Those drives were sacred interludes for us—sometimes silent, sometimes graced by the Quran's soothing verses, or filled with my murmured prayers, broken into simple syllables for him to echo, even as my own thoughts wandered in divine reverie.

The therapy unfolded without alarm, a playful bridge to expression. But after a few sessions, the therapist presented a questionnaire—a seemingly straightforward scale assessing behaviours and milestones. We answered swiftly, my heart unburdened; if a query prompted pause or hazy recollection, it earned a lower mark, a fleeting shadow I dismissed. Little did I know it was the first of countless forms that would punctuate our path, each one a quiet harbinger of the revelations to come.

A week later, the call arrived: Ilyas required more—occupational therapy alongside speech. My husband relayed the news while I sat at my desk, ensnared in work's demands. "Occupational therapy?" I echoed, my mind drifting to workplace health protocols, not the tender needs of a toddler. We deferred the discussion to evening's calm. They recommended two clinics; one aligned with our insurance, a practical mercy amid the mounting costs we'd already shouldered in cash. The assessment appointment loomed, a fraught ordeal where Ilyas, deprived of his nap to fit their rigid schedule, resisted with every fibre of his being. I pleaded over the phone for earlier slots, voicing the injustice of setting him up for failure, but my concerns dissolved into the ether. To them, it seemed a mere formality—a checkbox for coverage, a transaction in a system where profit eclipsed empathy. We pressed on, oblivious to the word "autism," our minds unclouded by its shadow. Born amid COVID's isolation, with both parents tethered to full-time work, Ilyas's world felt confined; we assumed therapy would simply fill his days with purpose, yielding steady blooms of progress. How could we have known that this was merely the prelude to a deeper awakening, one that would test the very fabric of our acceptance and love?

ARE WE ACCEPTING?

Echoes of Denial: A Stranger's Sting and the Gathering Storm

The whisper of "autism" first pierced my world not from a doctor's sterile decree, but from the lips of a stranger—a woman auditioning as our nanny, her words landing like a venomous dart in the fragile armour of my denial. It was late January 2022, and as I bid her farewell after a three-day trial in our home, she paused at the door, her voice casual yet cutting: "Your son is autistic; he needs special attention." My blood ran cold. How dare she—a fleeting presence in our lives—brand my precious Ilyas with such a label, as if to secure her position by exploiting my deepest fears? I dismissed her outright, branding her rude, opportunistic, her "observation" a slanderous ploy. Why withhold it during those days she shadowed us, if it stemmed from genuine concern? Rage simmered within me, a mother's fierce protectiveness shielding me from the truth she dangled.

That same week, Ilyas turned two—a milestone eclipsed by illness, his birthday swallowed by COVID's grip, with his father confined in isolation. No cake, no laughter; just the quiet ache of a family weathering yet another storm, oblivious to the greater tempest brewing.

As winter softened, we ventured deeper into therapy at Clinic #2, a sanctuary for speech and occupational sessions that promised to unlock Ilyas's voice. The speech therapist was a force of nature—vibrant, booming, her face a canvas of exaggerated expressions that filled the hallways with life, drawing every child into her orbit. She was a beacon, her energy a balm for my weary heart. But the occupational therapist? A stark contrast—languid, almost detached, her sessions lacking the vigour needed to engage a child's senses and movements. From the very first encounter, she urged applied behavioural analysis (ABA) therapy, her recommendation feeling premature, a hasty deflection before she'd even glimpsed Ilyas's full potential. We bristled—partly at the added burden, uncovered by insurance, but mostly at her perceived laziness, pushing us toward another path without first earning our trust. We delayed, clinging to the hope that time and our current efforts would suffice.

By early 2022, our lives shifted to a spacious new home in Baniyas, the drive to Clinic #2 stretching to forty-two minutes of winding roads. My family's driver became our lifeline, ferrying Ilyas to his twice-weekly back-to-back sessions on Sundays, turning them into family outings amid the city's hum. Yet, as Ilyas passed two years old, we sought more structure, enrolling him in a second nursery—a Montessori-inspired haven, though not the city's most renowned. We'd toured it together, letting him explore the classrooms while we weighed the costs. At first, it seemed idyllic: I dropped him off each morning, his afternoons split between my mother's warmth or therapy, with some days dedicated solely to healing. But shadows crept in. Three weeks later, drop-offs dissolved into tears, triggered by a new assistant teacher whose presence unsettled him. I voiced my worries, receiving assurances that his beloved teacher would remain close—promises that rang hollow in the classroom's reality.

Regression followed like a thief in the night. Ilyas, once curious and contained, began scavenging the floor for scraps—dust, crumbs, anything to chew—a habit that worsened with nursery exposure. My heart twisted at the daily photos: no smiles, only furrowed brows and confusion, echoes of his first nursery fiasco on Reem Island, where unrelenting cries had forced us to withdraw after a single week. No mother can peer behind those closed doors, and reassurances from staff felt like fragile veils over unspoken truths. We endured four months—one full term and a faltering start to the next—before I pulled him out, my instincts screaming that this "enriching" environment was eroding him instead. Child exposure, I had believed, could only nurture; yet here was proof of its double edge, a principal I'd clung to blindly, delaying the acknowledgment that Ilyas's world demanded more nuanced care.

Mid-year break arrived as a reprieve, and with it, our tentative embrace of ABA therapy. We bid the nursery farewell, welcoming winter's pause with a fresh routine—two weeks to test these new waters, hoping they might stem the tide of regression. In those moments, doubt gnawed at me: Had I delayed too long, shielding my heart from the word "autism" that strangers and signs had begun to murmur? Each tear, each unexplained habit, was a silent plea, pulling me toward acceptance—not as surrender, but as the fierce love that would redefine us both, weaving our story into a tapestry of resilience for a world that so desperately needs to see.

The young ABA therapist from Clinic #2 burst into our lives like a whirlwind of joy—vibrant, playful, her energy a spark that ignited something deep within Ilyas's guarded world. We adored her from the start, and over time, she transcended her role, becoming woven into our family fabric as she transitioned to home sessions, her laughter echoing through our rooms like a cherished melody. Back in 2022's mid-year break from nursery, we invested in two weeks of intensive therapy—two hours daily for nine days, a rhythm we hoped would recalibrate his behaviours, a corrective surge amid the uncertainty. It felt monumental, this commitment, and buoyed by early glimpses of progress, we extended it: another package of ten or sixteen hours, stretched across weeks like a lifeline, interwoven with speech, occupational therapy, and nursery days. It was a mosaic of efforts, a cocktail of hope and exhaustion, as we balanced healing with the simple act of letting him be a child.

I worked from home that first day of the new nursery term, savouring the quiet moments to reinforce what the therapist had taught—those subtle cues and reinforcements that had begun to bridge the chasms in our communication. When Ilyas returned, I helped him shed his clothes, settling him with tender care before offering a snack. But in an instant, the air shifted: he flung the food away with a guttural grunt, a raw, defiant sound that pierced my soul like a stranger's cry. This wasn't my boy—the one who'd meet my eyes, handing back unwanted bites with gentle protest. No, this was regression, a heartbreaking slide backward after those precious ABA strides. My heart clenched; something in that nursery had unravelled him, a thread pulled loose in the fabric of his fragile trust.

The signs mounted like storm clouds. His newfound obsession with scavenging the floor—dust, crumbs, invisible specks he chewed relentlessly—worsened with each nursery visit, a compulsion that twisted my gut with worry. I clung to the belief that exposure to peers would nurture him, blind to the irony: Montessori's ethos of independent exploration, so lauded for typical children, proved a silent trap for my son. Left to his own devices in that "free" environment, he withdrew into isolation, his world shrinking to solitary echoes. The Arabic term for autism, "tawahhud," derives from "wahad"—one, alone—and in those moments, I envisioned him adrift on those dusty carpets, overlooked, misunderstood, his spirit curling inward while no one truly saw him. Even I, his mother, hadn't yet uttered the word "autism," my denial a veil over the truth, leaving us all in the dark—therapists prescribing routines, teachers enforcing independence, family offering well-meaning but incomplete support.

Fractured Trust: A Mother's Stand and the Summer of Gentle Renewal

I persisted, paying the term in full, engaging the teachers in earnest dialogues, desperate for answers. But when a runny nose struck—mild, no fever—I sent extra bibs, trusting they'd tend to him. The family driver, a steadfast presence in our lives for years, collected him that afternoon and recounted a scene that shattered me: dried mucus crusted across his cheeks and mouth, his face a map of discomfort, exhaustion etching lines on his tender skin. He'd cleaned Ilyas himself in the car, a quiet act of compassion that spoke volumes. The next day, I kept Ilyas home to recover, sending a note to the nursery. Midday, the senior administrator called, her voice laced with feigned concern. I broached the issue gently—"Perhaps the assistants were overwhelmed with his nose?"—but she dismissed it airily: "He was fine, calmer even." Pressing further, insisting on the delay in his healing from neglect, she snapped, "Why would I listen to a driver?" The words landed like a blow, my shock rendering me speechless, eyes wide in disbelief.

"Yes," I retorted, my voice steady despite the tremor in my chest, "I will listen to him—he's been with us for years, caring for Ilyas with more devotion than anyone at your nursery." That was the final unravelling. Refund or not (and there was none), I withdrew him, attending a few more days to ease the transition, preserving ties in our shared community. We are all threads in the same fabric, after all; perhaps that was the best they could offer, their limitations a mirror to my own lingering denial. But in pulling him free, my heart wept for the lost innocence, the unseen wounds inflicted by a system blind to his needs—a poignant reminder that acceptance begins not in grand gestures, but in the quiet courage to see, to protect, and to choose love over convenience.

ARE WE ACCEPTING?

With the nursery doors closed behind us, a fragile peace descended on our home—a deliberate pause in Ilyas's whirlwind schedule, granting him the gift of lighter days until summer camp beckoned. His weeks unfolded in gentle rhythms: visits to his grandmother's welcoming arms, where stories and laughter flowed like warm tea, or excursions to his therapists—twice-weekly dives into occupational and speech sessions, punctuated by a single ABA encounter. It was a balm for his spirit and mine, allowing breaths of normalcy amid the storm of uncertainty.

As the summer's heat enveloped Abu Dhabi, we ventured to Nursery #3, our neighbourhood haven teeming with Arab and Emirati children whose vibrant energy mirrored our cultural heartbeat. They were a whirlwind of expression—boisterous, playful, perhaps a touch fierce, but always rooted in purehearted camaraderie, drawing everyone into their joyful orbit. For Ilyas, it was a revelation; this shift sparked subtle blooms in his wellbeing, his eyes brighter, his steps surer. We eased him in with tender care: two hours on alternate days at first, granting home or therapy respites on others. Week by week, we layered on more—extending hours, adding days—until, by the fifth week, he embraced all five days with a budding confidence we'd nurtured like a fragile seedling. This gradual ascent allowed us to watch for shadows—any flicker of discomfort or fear—that might disrupt his fragile equilibrium. Nurseries should be sanctuaries of delight, where young souls entwine in shared wonder, yet too often, unspoken anxieties lurk: a strange corner that frightens, an unfamiliar face that unsettles.

Parents and teachers alike must remain vigilant, carving space to unravel these hidden threads, for only then can joy truly flourish. Ilyas's summer start, with fewer peers crowding the rooms, gifted his teachers the intimacy to connect deeply—a quiet grace that eased his integration.

From Shadows to Light: Embracing Acceptance Beyond Denial

Yet, beneath this fragile harmony, the doctor's words from Clinic #2 haunted us that sweltering summer of 2022. Amid Ilyas's "cocktail" of therapies—OT, ST, ABA weaving a tapestry of support—she summoned us, her voice steady: "It's time for the autism assessment." My heart recoiled. "No," I whispered, the word a shield against the abyss. "Wait—could he be autistic? But he is me, as I was—a dreamer lost in wonder—and I turned out fine."

Oh, how I saw my own childhood echoing in him: those distant gazes into nothingness, where the world blurred and imagination reigned. I'd lean close, aligning my eyes with his, peering into the void he fixated upon, conjuring what visions danced in his mind. It transported me to little Hanoona—the girl I once was—a silent observer in kindergarten, watching peers frolic while my head brimmed with unspoken riddles. Others blurted "Why?" like arrows into the air, but I pondered in solitude, unravelling answers like threads from a spool. One puzzle lingered longest: why did clothes shrink? Mother would dress me, sighing in Arabic, "Your pants have shrunk again." We'd venture to the shop for replacements, and they'd fit perfectly there—but homeward, they'd betray me. Was it the store's magic, holding them steady? The air conditioning's chill? No, we had that at home. The cupboards, perhaps, squeezing them tight while shop displays breathed free? For a week, it consumed me, until epiphany struck: it wasn't the clothes diminishing, but me expanding, growing beyond their grasp. I was nearly four, and Mother had hoped my kindergarten PE pants would stretch into the new year. In Ilyas's daydreams, I saw that same introspective spark—my own undiagnosed echoes, perhaps—and it fortified my denial: if I had thrived, so would he.

The possibility clawed at me, elusive and terrifying. The doctors and therapists, after eight months of intimate sessions, likely saw the signs in his stalled progress, but as his mother, I framed his challenges as ordinary rites—the wild energy of boyhood, the primitive urges of youth. Speech delay was my sole foe; let's arm him with words, I thought, and all would align. I bargained with the doctor: "Continue the therapies; give him time to bloom. We'll revisit the assessment if—when—we must."

Home became a cauldron of chaos, frustrations boiling over as our silent voids widened. A toddler without words forges his own language—and for Ilyas, it was the insistent grasp of my hand, a desperate bridge to his needs. At first, we misread it, lost in ignorance, his cries a torrent of unexplained pain that mirrored my own helplessness, reducing us both to tears. One evening, as I chopped vegetables for dinner, Ilyas played on his mat, toys scattered like forgotten dreams, his water bottle within reach. He'd tug at my leg, pull my pants, but I'd glance down absently, assuring myself he was fine, my focus tethered to the meal. Moments later, his father slipped out for a delivery—and Ilyas shattered the air with sudden wails, raw and piercing, sending me into panic. Had he hurt himself? I scooped him up, hugged fiercely, offered water, sang lullabies—but the storm raged on. Only when his father returned did silence descend, the truth dawning: abandonment's sting, his dad's exit leaving him adrift with a mother too distracted to see. We marvelled at the oversight, yet frustration lingered—why couldn't he simply tell us?

That night unlocked a floodgate, illuminating past screams as "tantrums"—eruptions in malls, streets, hospitals, cars, family gatherings—mysteries that had baffled and broken me. How many had I endured blindly? I turned to my husband, voice trembling: "Okay, our son is autistic. Let's seek treatment, move past this chaos, quieten the screams at home."

But there was no "moving past." Autism demanded more—a labyrinth of knowledge, education, training, and acceptance, acceptance, acceptance. Thrice-fold, for its essence shifts like desert sands: no two souls alike, no single journey static—from childhood's innocence to adolescence's storms, into adulthood's uncharted horizons. In denying it, I'd shielded my heart; in embracing it, I found the courage to rewrite our story, one of love's unyielding light.

Embracing Without Shadows: The True Essence of Acceptance

In the quiet recesses of my heart, where the raw edges of motherhood meet the vast unknown of raising my autistic son, Ilyas, acceptance has become more than a word—it's a lifeline, a deliberate choice woven into the fabric of our days. At its core, acceptance means opening ourselves to something or someone with a willing heart, acknowledging their reality or truth without resistance. In the realm of psychology, it deepens into a profound embrace: welcoming thoughts, feelings, and experiences without the sting of judgement, allowing emotions to flow freely like a desert stream after rain. And oh, how I cherish this extension—that acceptance is to regard something as utterly normal, stripping away the veils of "otherness" that society so often drapes over those who diverge from its narrow norms. For me, as an autistic mother navigating this path, and for countless families touched by disability—visible or veiled—we've too often been cast adrift from the shores of "normal," labelled as exceptions rather than equals, our stories sidelined in a world that craves conformity.

I confess, acceptance didn't dawn gently for me; it arrived after a fierce tussle with denial, a shadow that cloaked my vision when Ilyas's autism first whispered its presence. How could

I embrace what I scarcely understood? Autism, after all, is a hidden disability—a subtle mosaic of developmental delays and neural differences that defies easy detection. Unlike conditions with more overt markers, such as Down syndrome or the absence of a sense, autism unfolds in the quiet intricacies of the brain: a unique wiring that shapes perception, communication, and connection in ways the world often misreads. Many, like me in those early days, remain unaware of its nuances—seeing only the surface ripples, not the profound depths beneath. Yet, in learning to accept, I've discovered a transformative power: it invites society to widen its embrace, fostering inclusion where judgement once reigned, ensuring that every individual, neurodivergent or otherwise, is seen not as a puzzle to solve, but as a vital thread in humanity's rich tapestry.

Redefining "Normal": Practical Steps Toward Heartfelt Acceptance

In the tender quiet of my reflections as Ilyas's mother, I've come to see "normal" not as a benevolent standard, but as a constructed cage—a normative lens that casts differences as flaws, disabling individuals through rigid designs and unforgiving labels that society clings to like outdated maps. From the neurodivergent perspective, it's a myth we must dismantle, one that overlooks the vibrant spectrum of human experience, turning strengths into shadows and uniqueness into isolation. Oh, how this realisation pierced me during those early days of denial when I wrestled with Ilyas's world, fearing the word "autism" would exile us from the "normal" I once chased. Yet, in embracing it, I've learned acceptance isn't passive surrender; it's an active, courageous rewiring of our hearts and minds, inviting society to expand its embrace. To challenge this illusion and foster true inclusion, let's walk through these three gentle yet transformative steps together, steps that have guided me from heartache to hope, weaving empathy into the fabric of our shared humanity.

Step 1: Interrogate Your Inner Narratives.
Begin by pausing to examine the images you've internalised—of "normal" as a polished ideal versus neurodivergence as a deviation. Suspend those biases, those whispered assumptions that whisper "less than," and open yourself to witnessing authentic capabilities blooming in their own time. For me, this meant confronting the mirror of my own childhood quirks—those zoned-out moments I once dismissed as daydreaming—and recognising them in Ilyas, not as deficits, but as portals to profound insight. It's a humbling unravelling, one that softens the heart, urging us to see every individual not through society's narrow prism, but in their full, radiant light.

Step 2: Illuminate the Gifts Within.
Pivot from the weary gaze of deficits to a celebration of strengths, honouring the unique talents that neurodivergent souls bring to our world. Shift your focus to what shines—the innovative perspectives, the unfiltered purity of thought that defies convention. Take Ilyas, for instance: in a bustling mall, he fixates not on the crowds or chaos, but on the automatic

doors, approaching them with relentless curiosity, retreating and advancing, peering at hinges and sensors as if unravelling the universe's secrets. He shakes his head at my explanations—"auto door, no touch"—insisting on his own comprehension, a testament to his brain's refusal to accept rote truths without deep understanding. In these moments, my eyes well with a mix of awe and tenderness; his "delays" are not absences but invitations to pause, to appreciate the unhurried wisdom that could teach society to question, to truly see beyond the superficial.

Step 3: Champion Transformation.
Finally, channel this awakening into advocacy, demanding environments that bend to accommodate differences rather than expel them. Reject the heartbreaking expulsions—for a diagnosis like autism or ADHD—that shatter families and stifle potential; instead, push for spaces where every child, every person, belongs without apology. In my journey, this meant advocating fiercely for Ilyas, from challenging nurseries that failed him to seeking therapies that honoured his pace, all while envisioning a society where inclusion isn't an afterthought but the foundation. It's a call to action born from love's quiet fire, one that echoes through our communities, building a world where no one is left on the margins, but all are woven into the beautiful, diverse tapestry of life.

Supporting Material
Use this bias checklist:

Assumption	Deficit View	Strength View	Action to Shift
Behaviour	Troublemaker	Unique expression	Observe patterns

For resources, read "The Myth of the Normal Brain" on journalofethics.ama-assn.org or "Neurodiversity and a Critique of the Concept of Normal" on medium.com

Beyond Denial: The Imperative of Embracing Neurodivergence

In the quiet depths of my heart, where the fierce love for my son Ilyas battles the world's unyielding expectations, I've come to understand that autism, ADHD, or any neurodivergence isn't the true challenge—it's our refusal to acknowledge them, to integrate them into what we deem "normal." How often have my family members, with the best of intentions, murmured, "There's nothing wrong with him," their words a gentle veil over the reality that pierces me like thorns? They mean to comfort, yet it stings, unfair to me as his mother and unjust to Ilyas himself. For there is nothing "wrong" with autism—nothing to fix or erase. He is autistic, a beautiful truth we cannot deny or wish away, hoping time will magically align him with society's narrow mould. As parents, we shoulder the profound weight of intervening, guiding him through life's labyrinth with therapies, advocacy, and unwavering presence.

But this burden shouldn't rest on us alone; our communities must awaken too, for every one of us—whether bound by blood or chance encounter—will cross paths with neurodivergent souls, and in those moments, understanding becomes our shared duty, a bridge to the inclusive world we all deserve.

When those dismissive phrases echo from loved ones, I steady my voice and correct them gently yet firmly, transforming each exchange into advocacy for autism's quiet power. "Yes, he's okay," I respond, my eyes meeting theirs with a mix of resolve and tenderness, "because autism is okay." But oh, how I yearn to unfold the layers beneath, to paint the full portrait of what "okay" truly entails in our hidden battles. Here, in these pages, I can elaborate, inviting society to listen and learn:

- **Yes, he's okay because autism is okay**—A spectrum of brilliance, not a flaw to mend, reminding us all that diversity enriches our humanity.
- **Yes, he's okay because of the unseen labours of his parents**—Endless nights of research, tears shed in solitude, and hearts poured into every decision, crafting a path where he can thrive.
- **Yes, he's okay because a dedicated team of professionals surrounds him**—Therapists observing with keen eyes, evaluating progress, and coaching us all, from parents to teachers, in the art of true support.
- **Yes, he's okay because reflection is our daily ritual**—Pausing at day's end to unravel moments, learning from stumbles and celebrating whispers of growth.

- **Yes, he's okay because he's enveloped in a community that remembers**—One I gently remind to grasp autism's multifaceted nature, fostering spaces where differences bloom without judgement.
- **Yes, he's okay because his mother challenged the giants**—Doctors, experts, and systems that faltered, advocating fiercely for what his soul truly needs.
- **Yes, he's okay because his shadow teacher stands empowered**—Equipped not just with tools, but with empathy, walking beside him as an ally in his unique journey.

And ultimately, yes, he's okay—perhaps even more so than us, the so-called "normal" ones, ensnared in society's invisible chains, our minds conditioned to conformity. In Ilyas's unfiltered gaze, I glimpse freedom: a purity that questions, resists, and redefines. By embracing neurodivergence without hesitation, we don't just heal families like mine—we liberate society itself, building a world where every individual, seen and unseen in their struggles, is honoured as essential, their light illuminating paths we never knew existed.

I love someone with autism and wish everyone this special kind of love. It's not a feeling; it's a generous act that grows every day. An active love based on care, responsibility, respect, and knowledge. It takes effort and time to learn, and we have to do it. It's unfair for neurodivergent children and adults to spend hours in clinical environments learning to live with neurotypical people when those people can't put in half the effort. Getting neurotypical, normal, individuals to put in an effort towards people of determination is advocating. Identify one "normal" assumption in your life and reframe it from a neurodivergent view.

There is an obvious need for understanding diverse abilities to build true inclusion. The next chapter discusses advocating efforts at an individual level and advocating at a community level in fun and informative ways.

8

ARE WE ADVOCATING?

Advocating for the unheard and amplifying voices for a world that embraces all

Imagine walking into a place meant for healing, only to find walls of indifference taller than any barrier your child already faces. For parents like me, advocacy isn't a choice—it's the lifeline that bridges the gap between a child's silent struggles and a society's slow awakening.

By the end of this chapter you will learn that advocacy is necessary and fun. Most advocacy is being conducted by caregivers of people with disabilities because they are suffering in daily lives with challenges and accessibility issues. As caregivers and parents, we do not even realise we are advocating until after an incident, after a heated argument where the "normal" staff could not comprehend an issue, or after applying for a request that is being rejected and following up with the contact centres puts us through repeated storytelling of our struggles. Gradually, this adds up. We need support to relieve the stress. Advocating will help us help our diverse-abled communities merge and will help us recharge our energies.

The Unheard Chords: A Mother's Heartbreak and Unyielding Advocacy in a World Blind to Neurodivergence

In the quiet chaos of raising a neurodivergent child, every outing becomes a battlefield—not against the child, but against a world that often forgets to see them. Neurodivergent children and adults navigate social life like sailors in a storm, their voices drowned out by waves of misunderstanding. They can't always explain why a simple process feels like an assault on their senses, or why overwhelming emotions erupt without warning. That's where we, the parents, step in—not as experts with degrees, but as fierce advocates armed with the deepest knowledge of all: lived experience. Our insights aren't theoretical; they're forged in the fire of countless trials, making us professionals in our own right. Yet, too often, we're dismissed, forcing us to fight harder, louder, for the accommodations our loved ones deserve. This is the story of one such day—a failed

ARE WE ADVOCATING?

EEG appointment that left me heartbroken but more determined than ever to advocate, because if I don't, who will?

It started with hope, as so many of these appointments do. Ilyas, my vibrant, non-verbal son on the autism spectrum, needed an EEG to rule out epileptic risks before starting Hyperbaric Oxygen Therapy (HBOT). The lead doctor had been clear: this scan was essential. Knowing Ilyas's heightened sensitivities—his brain wired differently, every sound amplified, every touch a potential trigger—I prepared meticulously. I administered melatonin syrup at 2:20 p.m. to help him sleep through the procedure, as wired awake would be impossible for him. We drove to the hospital, me chatting animatedly to keep him from dozing too soon, my heart pounding with the familiar mix of anxiety and resolve. By 2:50 p.m., we were parked; by 2:55 p.m., registered and waiting.

As Ilyas nestled into my lap, his eyelids heavy, I turned to the nurse with a plea born of experience: "Could we enter the room now, before he fully sleeps? It would help him settle on the bed comfortably." I knew this from endless therapies—transitions are everything for autistic children. But she brushed me off with a robotic smile: "The technician is preparing the machine." Preparing? As if glimpsing an "unready" room would shatter us. I bit back my frustration, but inside, I seethed. Why dismiss a mother's insight? I've lived Ilyas's world every day—his aversions to new environments, his need for gentle easing. This wasn't a whim; it was wisdom hard-won through tears and triumphs.

More waiting, more work on my part to soothe him. By 3:10 p.m., the technician finally called us in. I scooped up my sleeping boy, leaving our bags behind in a rush, my arms aching but my focus laser-sharp. Gently, I laid him on the bed...and he stirred. Awake now, in this sterile, unfamiliar space. My stomach dropped. I lay beside him, patting his back, humming softly—the rituals that calm his storms. Ten precious minutes ticked by as I coaxed him back to sleep, gesturing urgently for the technician to stay quiet. "He's autistic," I whispered when the moment allowed. "We have to be careful; he needs to stay asleep for the full 45 minutes." The file was there, the referral from neurodevelopmental paediatrics glaringly obvious, yet I had to explain, advocate, educate—again.

The technician began attaching wires, and I hovered close, murmuring Quran verses under my breath, praying for peace. Halfway done, we needed to turn Ilyas onto his back. One small movement—and his eyes flew open. Panic flooded his face: strange room, wires tangling like vines, betrayal in every sensation. He sat up, yanking at them, his body a whirlwind of distress. I tried to hold him, whispering, "It's okay, habibi, Mama's here," but trust was shattered. He bolted from the bed, teetering on the edge of tears, until I thrust his scooter forward—a lifeline to calm. He mounted it, zooming toward the door, wires dangling like forgotten promises.

Apologising to the technician felt hollow; this wasn't just a failed test—it was a failure of the system. "Note it as attempted," I said, my voice steady despite the ache in my chest. As we

ARE WE ADVOCATING?

left, Ilyas scooting ahead with innocent determination, I fantasised about wearing a billboard next time: "My Son is Autistic. Autism Means: His Brain Works Differently. His Senses Are Heightened. What's Innate for You Isn't Comprehensible for Him." Maybe then they'd listen. The hospital's streamlined protocols—efficient for "normal" patients—ignored the extra layers neurodivergent families navigate. Even finding the right zone required piecing together clues from janitors and guards, a scavenger hunt no one should endure. If neurotypical adults like me need clear directions, imagine the rehearsals our children require!

This wasn't isolated; it's the daily advocacy dance. In hospitals, schools, travel, sports—everywhere—Ilyas's world demands I speak up. From early interventions to swimming classes, we've leaned on the UAE's blessings: safe neighbourhoods, pristine parks, world-class hospitals drawing global experts, selective schools, thriving communities. Yet, even here, gaps persist, reminding me: advocacy never stops. Parents of neurodivergent children aren't just caregivers; we're warriors, our experiences a blueprint for change. We must persist—demanding rehearsals for procedures, empathy in waiting rooms, recognition that our "advice" is in fact expertise. Because when we advocate, we don't just help our child; we pave the way for an inclusive society where every voice, spoken or silent, is heard.

Living in the UAE amplifies this hope—services are within reach, challenges met with ambition to import the world's best. But true inclusion starts with listening to us, the parents who know. So, to every mother, father, caregiver: keep advocating. Your voice, emotional and unyielding, is the spark that ignites change. For Ilyas, for all of them—let's build a world that bends to understand, not break.

Everyday Advocacy: The Quiet Battles That Shape Inclusion

Advocacy isn't reserved for grand gestures or public forums—it's woven into the fabric of everyday life, a quiet yet fierce commitment that parents and caregivers of people with diverse abilities must embrace. It's the daily stand we take, armed not with placards but with our unyielding love, sharp observations, and the hard-earned wisdom from countless moments of trial and tenderness. For me, as Ilyas's mother, this means being fully present in every phase of his young life, offering sincere attention that sees beyond behaviours to the boy beneath, a meticulous follow-up that ensures no detail slips through the cracks, and the courage to share our experienced truths, even when they're met with scepticism. In these early years, my advocacy unfolds most often in the realms of education and healthcare, where early interventions promise progress but too often demand conformity at the expense of understanding.

Take, for instance, the therapists who labelled Ilyas 'stubborn' during sessions, their frustration evident as he resisted their structured play on a mat or within the confines of a padded room. My heart ached hearing those words—stubborn? No, I countered firmly, he simply knows what he wants, a profound self-awareness that outshines blind obedience. He senses when he's hungry or full, when he's reached his limit or can stretch a little further—intuitions that elude even some adults, lost in the noise of their own disconnected lives. Forcing compliance in such rigid settings might mould a child who nods along to authority, but it won't nurture the independent spirit we dream of for our children. I advocated not just for Ilyas but for a shift in perspective: let's celebrate his agency and guide it gently, rather than crush it under the weight of outdated expectations.

Then there were the teachers, well-meaning but insistent, who warned that without clearer speech, Ilyas might repeat kindergarten, stalling his journey to first grade. The pressure stung, evoking visions of my son sidelined while peers surged ahead, but I stood my ground with quiet resolve. "He does communicate," I explained, my voice steady yet laced with the emotion of a mother who has decoded his world syllable by syllable. "It's your turn to listen more deeply." Ilyas's words may emerge as whispers or what sounds like random noise to untrained ears—like "siya," his sweet shorthand for "sing," uttered with eyes sparkling as I hum a tune at home. "Yes, habibi," I'd respond, pulling him close, "Mama is singing. Shall we sing together?" In those moments, advocacy feels like a bridge, urging educators to expand their definition of language beyond perfect articulation to the rich, nuanced ways our children connect. It's a call to honour their voices, however they manifest, fostering inclusion rather than exclusion.

This philosophy echoes a timeless wisdom I've come to cherish: when a flower fails to bloom, we don't blame the petals—we mend the soil, adjust the sunlight, or repot it into a space where roots can thrive. The same holds true for our children and adults with diverse abilities. **Fix the environment, not the individual**. In Ilyas's case, that means challenging systems that overlook sensory needs, social cues, or emotional rhythms, and instead cultivating spaces where growth unfolds naturally. It's advocacy in action, emotional and relentless, because every unmet need is a silent plea we must amplify.

Even in subtler encounters, the fight persists. I recall a clinic where a specialist chided that Ilyas was "too pampered," implying my nurturing approach was a flaw, a barrier to his progress. The words landed like a blow, stirring a whirlwind of doubt and defensiveness—how dare they critique the love I pour into him, the same tenderness I extend to everyone in my life? "I pamper all those I hold dear," I replied, my tone resolute but laced with quiet fire, "and my son deserves every ounce of it." In their eyes, therapy demanded rigid obedience, a traditional mould that clashed with the gentle, responsive world I was building for him. I chose not to return, not out of spite, but out of a deep-seated conviction: true healing blooms in environments of love, not judgement. Advocacy, in that instance, was walking away—to seek allies who see the strength in softness, the power in patience.

These daily battles, though exhausting, are the heartbeat of change. They remind us that supporting people of determination isn't a passive role but an active, lifelong vow. As parents and caregivers, our voices—infused with the raw emotion of our journeys—pave the path toward a society that doesn't just accommodate but celebrates diversity. In every conversation, every correction, we plant seeds of empathy, urging the world to bloom alongside our loved ones.

Celebrating Advocacy: Turning Moments into Movements of Joy and Inclusion

Advocacy for neurodivergence extends far beyond the daily defences we mount as parents and caregivers—the vigilant corrections, the heartfelt explanations, the unyielding push for understanding. We stand as the unwavering front-line guardians for people of determination, but our role doesn't end in quiet battles; it blossoms into vibrant, exhilarating expressions that ignite change. Imagine transforming advocacy from a duty into a delight, seizing every glimmer of opportunity to illuminate autism and neurodivergence with warmth and wonder. There are endless windows to share stories, showcase strengths, and foster love for what makes us unique.

Recently, we embraced one such moment through Ilyas's fifth birthday, crafting a bespoke booklet that not only celebrated his milestone but invited his world to join in the joy.

This little treasure—a mere five content pages, each paired with an engaging activity—spoke from Ilyas's heart, weaving tales of his adventures while gently unveiling the essence of autism in simple, uplifting words. "Autism means my brain dances to its own rhythm," it might say, or "I see the world in brilliant colours and sounds—let's explore it together!" We distributed these booklets to his classmates and relatives, envisioning cozy evenings where children and parents read aloud, sparking curiosity and connection. The activities—puzzles mirroring sensory play, or prompts to share personal "superpowers"—turned learning into laughter, bridging gaps with play. It wasn't just a gift; it was an invitation to empathy, a spark that could light up young minds and ripple into families, schools, and beyond.

When you immerse yourself in this cause with genuine passion, the universe unfolds more paths, each one a canvas for creativity. Authoring that booklet ignited a cascade of ideas: interactive storybooks where neurodivergent heroes embark on quests tailored to diverse minds, or playful apps that gamify empathy-building for peers. These aren't mere whims; they're beacons of hope, proving that advocacy can be as joyful as it is transformative. By celebrating our children—people of determination, those with disabilities—we banish the shadows of shame and isolation. Too often, families retreat from gatherings or public spaces, daunted by the unpredictability of behaviours or the onslaught of sensory triggers. The mental load is immense: envisioning every potential meltdown, packing arsenals of comforts—multiple snacks for finicky appetites, a rotation of toys to redirect focus, or Ilyas's beloved scooter as a soothing escape when fidgetiness strikes. Yet, even with all this foresight, the moment might defy our plans, leaving us exhausted but undeterred.

Take our outings to theme parks, those glittering realms of wonder that, for us, demand a symphony of strategy and stamina. I prepare like a conductor, anticipating the highs and lows: coaxing Ilyas toward accessible rides while steering him from forbidden stairs or service doors that inexplicably captivate him. His fascination with entrances—swinging open and shut, automatic sliders ushering blasts of heat into cool sanctuaries—can disrupt the flow, drawing stares or sighs from others.

Guiding him away without sparking distress requires finesse: perhaps dangling a higher-value distraction, like a cherished toy, as a gentle pivot rather than a bribe. Then there's the siren call of others' food—pizza, his ultimate temptation, especially now on a gluten-free path. Spotting a slice, he'd dart toward it, arm outstretched in innocent yearning. We intercept swiftly, hearts racing, sometimes opting for a graceful exit to preserve peace. But here's the inspiration: we return, time and again. We embrace the challenges, arming ourselves with tools, honing our reflexes, and making serene decisions—like sensing the perfect pause for a quiet break. In these acts, we model resilience, teaching society that inclusion isn't flawless—it's fearless.

This is why, when the chance arises to orchestrate an event on your terms, infused with the neurodivergent individual's input, grasp it boldly. Invite the world—friends with and without disabilities, family near and far—to weave a tapestry of awareness and acceptance. Design with intention: opt for outdoor venues to soften echoing sounds, evening timings with soft, dimmed lights for a cocoon of calm over glaring hues. Keep crowds intimate or zone the space for gentle encounters, easing the overwhelm of a sea of faces. Curate the menu around safe, beloved foods—beige palettes for picky eaters, gluten-free delights, or ketogenic options—ensuring nourishment feels like nurture, not negotiation. And redefine the rhythm of celebration: a party needn't pulse with music and dance to thrum with life. Instead, envision a stage for a heartfelt play, the melodic recitation of Quran verses, or a circle of souls sharing stories—each turn prompting questions that draw out dreams, triumphs, and truths.

Whether marking a birthday, a first spoken word, a triumphant step off diapers, or a sibling's graduation, these gatherings become more than events—they're revolutions of the heart. They affirm that our loved ones deserve the spotlight, their journeys honoured with creativity and compassion. As a mother, I've felt the profound shift from isolation to invitation, from struggle to shared joy. Let this inspire you: advocacy, when infused with fun, doesn't just advocate—it *elevates*, uniting us in a symphony of inclusion where every voice, every difference, is a cause for celebration. Together, we build a society that dances to diverse rhythms, one joyful step at a time.

Occasions to accept and raise awareness of people with diverse-abilities:

- Celebrate neurodiversity week in March
- On Autism Awareness Day, April 2 and the entire month of April
- On Mother's Day, March 21 or the second Sunday of May, appreciating autism moms
- On Father's Day, the third Sunday of June, to appreciate the fathers of autistic children
- On World Friendship Day, July 30, to celebrate your love for someone with a diverse-ability
- International Literacy Day, September 8, to draw on the importance of reading and writing and face the challenges some individuals have due to dyslexia. Activities may include reading in different fonts, reading with coloured shades, writing using different pencil grips, or typing contests.
- International Day of sign Languages, September 23, to celebrate the deaf and hard-of-hearing individuals. This event is a chance to teach some sign language and make it into interactive play where attendees may guess the sentence being signed.
- On Teachers' Day, October 5, to acknowledge the efforts of shadow teachers
- Access Abilities Expo and other exhibitions such as book fair

- On your child's birthday: throw a party that caters to his/her needs and invite people so they learn more about you and others on the spectrum
- Back-to-school week: Prepare children to accept everyone's different abilities at class

What is the symbol for autism?

- The jigsaw puzzle piece
- The rainbow infinity
- The sunflower

Materials and content to use in celebration and awareness:

- Stickers with lovely messages and educational illustrations. If you cannot print stickers, try printing the symbols on a sheet of paper and turning it into an "I Spy" game
- Word Scramble game
- Canvases with a specific print on autism and watercolour paint
- Monochrome-coloured puzzle
- Scarves and earmuffs

Why Not: The Shadows of Conformity and the Courage to Challenge Them

Advocacy, at its core, is a profound opportunity to illuminate the essence of autism—to teach, to remind, to reclaim space in a world that too often demands uniformity. It's a gentle yet unyielding call to celebrate our differences, to shatter the illusion that we must all squeeze into society's narrow moulds. But why resist? Why not simply blend in, conform, and let the currents of "normalcy" carry us along? The answer lies in the quiet rebellion against a life scripted too rigidly, where sameness suffocates the soul.

In recent decades, we've all been funnelled into predictable cycles: childhood confined to classrooms where every student marches in lockstep, youth funnelled into professions that demand identical decorum, and senior years relegated to quiet retirement, fading into the background. Even our leisure bows to communal norms—the same shows, the same outings, the same scripted joys. We've become so "normal" that we've forgotten the beauty of divergence. It's time to advocate not just for the neurodivergent, but for the neurotypical too, awakening them from the trance of expecting everyone to mirror their own reflections. True inclusion blooms when we embrace the mosaic of humanity, not when we force every piece to fit the same puzzle.

This truth crystallised for me during a vibrant outing to Comic-Con, a whirlwind of colours, costumes, and creativity that should have been a playground for the unconventional. Ilyas, my spirited son, revelled in the ramps scattered everywhere, his scooter gliding like a superhero's cape in the wind. We paused for a time-out in the outdoor area—the best spot, alive with fresh air and open skies—where he discovered his own private adventure. In his brilliant mind, he'd mapped a perfect path: a subtle protrusion in the ground formed a smooth ramp right in front of a bustling food truck. Up and down he went, lost in the rhythmic joy of it, his laughter a silent melody amid the chaos. But this was no isolated bubble; people streamed across his route—passersby weaving through, others queued patiently for their bites. Ilyas, blissfully absorbed, paid them little heed, his scooter zipping straight into shins, reversing into unsuspecting backs, or innocently bumping over toes. The air hummed with potential mishaps, a delicate dance between his unfiltered delight and the world's unspoken rules.

In that moment, I chose to let it unfold, my heart a mix of protectiveness and curiosity. It was a test—not of Ilyas, but of humanity's capacity for grace. How would strangers respond to a child simply being a child, his autism weaving an unconventional thread into their orderly tapestry? One family melted my defences: they halted in their tracks, eyes wide with assumption that he was merely mastering his scooter, a novice in motion. As he whooshed past, they erupted in cheers, their voices a chorus of encouragement that lifted my spirit. "Go, little guy!" they called, transforming a potential disruption into a shared triumph. Yet, not all encounters were so seamless. When groups lingered in line, oblivious to his playful orbit, I'd approach with a warm smile, my voice steady yet laced with the quiet vulnerability of a mother advocating in real time. "He's found his perfect play path here," I'd explain gently, "and I'm so sorry if he bumps you—autism means his world spins a bit differently. If it's an annoyance, a simple step to the side would give him space without any fuss." Most nodded, shifted with kindness, their small concessions a ripple of understanding in a sea of sameness.

But advocacy isn't always smooth; it demands discernment, and I learned that the hard way once. In a flash of frustration—perhaps echoing the societal pressure to "correct" him—I chided Ilyas softly: "Watch the people around you, habibi; this might not be the best spot." His face crumpled, agitation flaring like a storm, his joy eclipsed. It wasn't the right time; teaching nuance amid the din would take patient practice, not a hurried reprimand. Why burden him, I realised, when the world around us brimmed with capable adults? They, the neurotypicals with honed social skills, could grasp a simple explanation far easier than my son could navigate the cacophony assaulting his senses—the blaring music, the chaotic chatter, the overwhelming buzz that drowned his auditory focus. For Ilyas, that scooter ride was sanctuary, a soothing ritual to steady his inner world. Placing the onus on him to adapt, to conform, felt not just unfair but profoundly misguided. Why not turn to those with the tools to understand, to adjust with empathy? In a society that prizes sameness, it's the "normal" who must stretch, learning that true harmony arises not from uniformity, but from the graceful accommodation of our beautiful differences.

These moments, emotional and raw, underscore the "why not" of advocacy: because without it, we perpetuate a world where expectations of normalcy stifle the extraordinary. Ilyas's playful disruptions weren't defiance; they were declarations of his unique rhythm. By advocating—through stories, smiles, and steadfast presence—we don't just protect our loved ones; we invite society to evolve, to cherish the diversity that makes us human. In the end, it's not about fitting in; it's about expanding the circle until everyone belongs.

Speaking up for people of determination, or people with disabilities/diverse-abilities, is a task for all of us. We are all connected to someone who is diverse and if not, then our communities benefit from being inclusive. Next time you are at the office and spot someone with a diverse-ability, approach them and speak to them to listen to their story and learn if there's a struggle you can help with. Diverse-abilities are everywhere, and our societies need to invite them to mingle and merge. There is no need for the wheelchair to feel out of place, the autism mum to tame her child, the blind to be cobbled. The next chapter talks about how we make this mingling seamless.

9

ARE WE INCLUSIVE?

Building ecosystems that honour all abilities

If we create disability through poor design, what would society look like if we centred people of determination in every space, service, and decision? Let us end the separation of normal from diverse-abilities so that societies are truly inclusive.

This chapter will enable us to empathise with diverse-abilities individuals at various stages of community building: in the early stages of childcare and education, in later stages of employability in office spaces, and throughout accessibility to public spaces. We will define inclusion as removing barriers for people of determination (PODs), using empathy and design to ensure full participation while drawing from my advocacy for Ilyas. In the process, you will learn how to create transformative ecosystems focused on strengths. By the end of this chapter, you will be able to apply inclusion principles in your community, contributing to happy families and open societies free from 'normal' constraints.

Threads of Exclusion: From Ancient Unity to the Hidden Brilliance of Neurodivergence

From the dawn of human history, civilisations have emerged not as mere accidents of fate, but as deliberate constructs shaped by the collective will to organise, survive, and thrive. In the cradle of ancient societies—be it the fertile valleys of Mesopotamia, the Nile's life-giving banks, or the vast steppes of early nomadic tribes—leaders recognised the necessity of unity amid growing populations. As clans swelled into cities and empires, the raw chaos of individual freedoms gave way to structured harmony. Religions first provided the moral compass, embedding shared values like compassion, justice, and communal responsibility into the fabric of daily life. Yet, as populations burgeoned and settlements rooted firmly in place, these spiritual guidelines evolved into man-made laws—rigid frameworks designed to shepherd the masses, ensuring order through control. What began as organic regulators of harmonious living—values passed down through heritage, religion, or nomadic wisdom—transformed into tools of governance, prioritising the disciplined nation over the untamed individual. In this shift, the emphasis on conformity eclipsed diversity, stifling voices that deviated from the norm and laying the groundwork for exclusion that persists to this day.

Yet, woven into this tapestry of control are threads of brilliance from those who defied the mould—individuals whose neurodivergent minds, often speculated or confirmed to align with autism, propelled humanity forward. Consider Albert Einstein, the revolutionary physicist whose theory of relativity reshaped our understanding of the universe; whispers of his childhood—marked by delayed speech, intense focus on complex ideas, and social withdrawal—suggest an autistic wiring that fuelled his unparalleled genius, allowing him to envision concepts others deemed impossible. Or Temple Grandin, the trailblazing animal scientist and autism advocate, whose hypersensitivity to sensory details revolutionised livestock handling systems, making them more humane and efficient; her autistic perspective, with its visual thinking and empathy for animal distress, turned perceived "limitations" into transformative innovations. Then there's Satoshi Tajiri, the creator of Pokémon, whose childhood fascination with collecting insects—stemming from his Asperger's syndrome—birthed a global phenomenon that blends strategy, exploration, and connection, captivating millions and subtly teaching empathy across generations. History brims with such luminaries: Nikola Tesla, the inventor whose obsessive focus and sensory sensitivities sparked electrical marvels; Hans Christian

Andersen, whose fairy tales captured the world's imagination through his profound introspection and social quirks; even Michelangelo, whose masterful sculptures and paintings may have drawn from an autistic intensity that isolated him yet amplified his vision. These figures, often misunderstood in their time, underscore a profound truth: neurodivergence is not a flaw to be erased but a catalyst for progress, challenging the very systems that sought to constrain them.

Echoes of Responsibility: Building Beyond the Book

As this book draws to its close, we stand at a threshold—not of farewell, but of renewed commitment. Each of us, whether as parents, educators, or stewards of society, bears the mantle to continually define ourselves as vital building blocks in our communities and the wider world. Yet, society, moulded over centuries and accelerated through industrialisation's forge, has often diminished the individual's worth, prioritising conformity over the rich mosaic of human potential.

In antiquity, before the gears of industry churned, civilisations expanded through organic bonds, where leaders guided with a shepherd's care, easing the burdens of growth. Values—those innate compasses of harmony—emerged from religion, heritage, or nomadic wisdom, allowing diverse souls to coexist in mutual respect. But as populations surged and nomads anchored to fixed lands, control supplanted collaboration:

religions formalised into doctrines, evolving into man-made laws that regimented behaviour, enforcing discipline at the expense of individuality. We were schooled to revere these edicts, yet in their rigidity, they often silenced the unique—stifling the daydreamers, the sensitive, the neurodivergent whose unconventional minds held the keys to innovation.

The odyssey of civilisation, fraught with triumphs and trials, owes its luminosity to those enigmatic figures who etched their legacies despite the shadows of misunderstanding. Take Einstein, dispatched from school with a damning note deeming him "incapable," only to redefine reality itself—his speculated autism a forge for brilliance that shattered conventional bounds. These stories remind us: progress blooms not from uniformity, but from embracing the extraordinary within the "atypical."

And here lies our climaxing call: in a world that has long undervalued the individual, let us reclaim our agency. Practice the traits we've explored—observe with empathy, sense the unspoken, reflect with intention—and extend them outward, advocating for spaces where neurodivergence thrives not in spite of, but *because* of, its difference. As a mother to Ilyas, I've learned this truth viscerally: when we build ourselves as inclusive units, we don't just mend families—we reconstruct society, one compassionate act at a time, ensuring no one is left at the margins. Your role begins now: carry this forward, and watch the world transform.

What Constitutes an Inclusive Society

An inclusive society is one that transcends mere tolerance, embracing the full spectrum of human diversity without erecting barriers between the "normal" and those with disabilities or diverse-abilities. It is a framework where every individual—regardless of physical, developmental, or neurodivergent traits—is afforded equitable access to opportunities, resources, and respect, fostering environments that adapt to needs rather than demanding conformity. In such a society, separation dissolves: neurotypical and neurodivergent individuals coexist as equals, their unique contributions valued not despite differences, but because of them. This vision demands systemic empathy—from accessible public spaces and digital services to workplaces and communities that prioritise strengths over labels—ensuring no one is marginalised or "othered." For families like mine, raising a child like Ilyas, inclusion means a world where autism is not a hurdle to overcome, but a natural variation that enriches the collective human experience.

Yet, to build this ideal, we must confront the enigmas at its core: what gives rise to autism and other neurodivergent traits? The origins remain shrouded in mystery, a complex interplay of factors that elude definitive explanation. Genetic predispositions may play a role, as evidenced by familial patterns and hereditary studies, while epigenetic influences—subtle modifications to gene expression triggered by environmental cues—add layers of intrigue. These could stem from prenatal

ARE WE INCLUSIVE?

exposures, dietary habits, or even stressors during critical developmental windows.

Environmental elements, such as toxins or nutritional deficiencies, have been scrutinised, alongside the possibility of heightened diagnostic awareness inflating prevalence rates. In my own reflection, I sense a genetic echo in our lineage—traits that mirror my childhood quirks, now reframed through the lens of autism. Recalling my early years, I was the quiet dreamer, zoning out in serene detachment; my mother recounts how, as a toddler, she could clean the entire apartment while I sat motionless in a corner, lost in my inner world. A genome sequencing for Ilyas returned negative for abnormalities, yet epigenetics whispers possibilities: changes wrought by my stressful delivery, the processed foods that laced our diets, or the vaccinations we dutifully received—including a flu shot at six months pregnant. Each thread tugs at the heart, a tapestry of "what ifs" that once consumed me.

But does unravelling the cause truly matter? In the grand arc of human evolution, no—for autism and its kin have always woven through our species' fabric, undiagnosed yet enduring, propelling innovation in societies past and present. These traits, far from anomalies to eradicate, may be nature's safeguard, ensuring diversity that fuels adaptation and progress. Without them, humanity's story would dim; they are not defects to "cure," but evolutionary imperatives that persist because they must. The climax of this inquiry lies not in blame or fixation on origins, but in release. For families, chasing causes devolves into futile accusations—whose genes falter? Why did one child regress post-vaccination while siblings thrived? Such pursuits fracture bonds, diverting energy from what heals: acceptance. In embracing Ilyas's autism without the shadow of causation, we free ourselves to advocate, innovate, and include—transforming personal pain into societal strength, where diverse-abilities are not burdens, but the very essence of our shared resilience.

Forging Forward: Our Collective Duty

As this book draws to a close, we arrive at a pivotal imperative: each of us must commit to perpetual self-building, positioning ourselves as indispensable units—the building blocks—of vibrant communities and resilient societies. Over decades, and indeed centuries, societal structures have been forged in ways that often subordinate the individual to the collective machine, prioritising uniformity over unique potential. Yet, by embracing the practices herein—observing with empathy, sensing unspoken needs, reflecting with intention—we reclaim our agency, ensuring that neurodivergence and diverse-abilities are not sidelined but celebrated as catalysts for progress. In this professional pursuit of inclusion, let us advocate tirelessly, educate purposefully, and integrate holistically, honouring the contributions of all. For in doing so, we not only elevate families like mine but fortify the human enterprise, culminating in a world where every voice, every ability, propels us toward harmony and innovation.

Embracing Double Empathy: Sharing the Burden of Understanding

The journey toward inclusion begins with double empathy—a profound recognition that the onus of adaptation should not fall solely on those with diverse-abilities. Why must individuals with disabilities or neurodivergence bear the full weight of fitting into a world designed without them in mind? From learning sign language to navigate silence to discerning traffic lights through colourblind lenses, the expectation is often one-sided, demanding extraordinary effort from the marginalised while the majority remains complacent. True inclusion flips this script: it invites neurotypical individuals to step forward, volunteering their time to assist People of Determination (PODs) and immersing themselves in their realities. Imagine placing yourself in their shoes—feeling the frustration of unaccommodated needs, the isolation of unspoken barriers. This act fosters gratitude for our own privileges, even the involuntary functions of our bodies we take for granted, like articulating thoughts trapped in the mind. Corporations can lead by mandating online training modules that illuminate the spectrum of diverse abilities, not merely defining terms but vividly illustrating how life unfolds differently through varied lenses of mind and body. Such education cultivates a workforce attuned to empathy, transforming workplaces into beacons of mutual respect where no one is left to bridge the gap alone.

Designing Empathic Spaces: Where Everyone Belongs

At the heart of inclusion lies the creation of spaces that anticipate and honour diverse needs, ensuring every individual feels seen and valued from the outset. This demands a paradigm shift: involving PODs as equal partners in the design process, their lived experiences guiding architects, educators, and planners to craft environments that adapt to humanity's full spectrum. Empathy is the cornerstone—suspending our assumptions to truly listen, respecting a child's "no" not as defiance but as a boundary to honour, as Loris Malaguzzi reminds us: "Creativity becomes more visible when adults try to be more attentive to the cognitive processes of children than to the results they achieve." In classrooms, for instance, rethink the hidden cubbies draped in fabric; curiosity will prevail, drawing children to explore what lies beneath. Instead, store non-child materials out of sight, freeing spaces for safe discovery. Consider the child's perspective: shelves as mountains to conquer, not forbidden territories. Overwhelmed by sensory stimuli in mainstream settings? Discard the "calming chair"—an isolating time-out that amplifies scrutiny—and introduce cozy nooks integrated into the ecosystem. These havens offer refuge without removal, allowing repositioning for self-regulation while remaining part of the group. Distribute them abundantly, empowering children to seek solitude, read, or connect in smaller circles—fostering belonging through thoughtful, inclusive design.

Child's/ Caretaker's perspective	Educator/ Caregiver's perspective	Ecosystem's perspective
I am motivated by my interests and ideas	I am intentional about selecting and offering play opportunities to children	Aesthetically inviting environment; the physical environment of light and noise might be causing challenging behaviours.
I use questions to engage my curiosity	I use critical reflection in my practice	Offer a sense of belonging by supporting children's identities and cultures.
I must test to make meaning and find evidence	I research new knowledge and information	Invite children to represent and make meaning of their world.
I can reason and be a creative problem-solver to reach a conclusion	I embrace and engage in perspective-changing through observation	Encourage children to wonder, research, test and explore their ideas.
I can argue my perspective and present the evidence to support it	I thoughtfully plan to provoke, inspire and captivate children's curiosity.	Spaces that promote collaboration, observation, and communication organised for accessibility and engagement.

Resources: "Disability Is Diversity" on learningforjustice.org, "Disability Inclusion" on cdc.gov, "What We Mean When We Talk About Inclusion" on communityinclusion.org

Perspectives in Harmony: From Caretaker to Ecosystem

Inclusion thrives when we harmonise viewpoints—from the caretaker's intimate lens, to the caregiver's supportive gaze, to the ecosystem's overarching embrace—ensuring no voice is silenced. The caretaker, often a parent like myself navigating Ilyas's world, brings firsthand insight into daily nuances. Caregivers—therapists, educators—offer specialised tools, while the ecosystem—schools, communities—provides the structural foundation. This triad demands collaboration: suspending biases to see PODs authentically, not as deficits or superheroes, but as capable individuals with identities, ideas, and interests. Professor Deborah J. Gallagher's wisdom resonates: disability is a "cultural construct," an interpretation of differences through normative filters. We create disability via inaccessible designs—unyielding environments that disable rather than enable. Shift the focus: centre PODs in every blueprint, prioritising strengths over labels. For play areas, malls, or hospitals, ask: how do we accommodate diverse abilities first? Ramps in plain view, not hidden; noise-dampening options like earmuffs; receptionists trained for varied communication needs. Appoint government case managers to guide PODs through services, shielding from exploitation amid social media's dubious cures. In my quest for stem cell therapy since 2022, I consulted Abu Dhabi doctors (one a study co-author), yet their pessimism and dismissals of global options ignored my anguish. This passion nearly led me astray to scams preying on desperate parents. Acceptance, bolstered by community, guards against such pitfalls—reminding us to embrace rather than "fix," for true inclusion blooms when we design with empathy at the core.

Seizing New Opportunities: Removing Barriers for All

The climax of inclusion lies in opportunity—dismantling obstacles so PODs access the world unhindered, their journeys seamless and empowered. Physical barriers are evident: a blind Muslim woman's path to a hospital stage, uncharted, forced her to grasp a stranger's arm despite religious tenets, her humour masking the indignity. Wheelchair users shouldn't prompt room rearrangements, spotlighting their needs; aesthetics must marry functionalities for all. Extend this to digital realms—passport renewals inaccessible to the blind, receptions mute to the deaf without interpreters, job hunts a labyrinth even for neurotypicals. PODs endure exhaustive preparations, a burden amplified for caregivers. Empathy demands we reimagine play areas functional for diverse abilities benefit every child; malls with turned-down noise or earmuffs offered; hospitals with versatile waiting areas. Government case managers could curate reliable services, countering social media's exploitative lures—like unverified stem cell promises that tempted my family, only to reveal doctors' biases and scams targeting vulnerability. Forgetting futile quests for "cures," we accept inclusion isn't charity but justice, where PODs thrive not despite differences, but through systems that honour them—culminating in a society where empathy isn't an afterthought, but the blueprint for progress.

The Barriers to Belonging: Why Inclusion Remains Elusive

In the pursuit of a truly inclusive society, we confront entrenched resistances that perpetuate division, often rooted in fear, inertia, and a reluctance to adapt. Many among us grapple with dismantling the invisible walls separating the "normal" from those with disabilities or diverse abilities, clinging to outdated norms that prioritise uniformity over humanity. Regrettably, this manifests in stark realities: schools that, upon receiving a diagnosis of autism or ADHD, expel children who were previously thriving—non-severe cases where parents are urged to disclose merely for awareness, only to face expulsion amid concerns of "unpredictable incidents." Such actions underscore a profound discomfort: the challenge of accepting that our own offspring might carry a disability, the logistical hurdles of erecting accessible amenities for the "less-abled," and the broader societal reluctance to decelerate our relentless pace, pausing to extend a hand to others. Yet, these "others" are not distant abstractions—they are our community, an intricate web that envelops us all, regardless of our differences, demanding we recognise our shared humanity.

My own awakening to this truth unfolded through quiet acts of advocacy for Ilyas, whose sensory world reshaped our everyday rituals. When supermarkets became battlegrounds of overwhelming lights and crowds, triggering his distress, I heeded his unspoken pleas—acknowledging his fears, validating his needs—and shifted our grocery rhythms to the open-air markets of our heritage. It was a simple pivot, yet transformative: no longer confined to sterile aisles, we immersed ourselves in the vibrant pulse of community life. Now, I know the baker's warm smile, the spices merchant's tales, the laundry man's quiet efficiency, even the tailor's steady hand. We linger to exchange greetings, even on days without purchases, forging bonds that nourish the soul. In these moments, Ilyas taught me a profound lesson: autistic and neurodivergent individuals are not the "weird" outliers ill-suited to our polished, systematised world. No—it is society that veers into strangeness, imposing a monotonous script where all must crave the same sustenance, chase identical dreams, and conform to uniform lives. We are force-fed this illusion, but our neurodivergent kin arrive as gentle disruptors, urging us to pause, decelerate, and rediscover what truly matters in our fragmented existence.

Neurodivergence embodies a purity of thought, untainted by rote acceptance, insisting on authentic comprehension over superficial compliance. When Ilyas grapples with a skill or milestone, I see not delay, but deliberation—his mind refusing to swallow information blindly, demanding to trace each step, to unravel the why. Take the automatic mall doors: he approaches, crosses, retreats, scrutinises the panels, gazes upward at their mechanisms, lingering for hours as crowds flow past. I describe—"auto door, no touch"—but he shakes his head in quiet dissent, rejecting my words until he deciphers the mystery himself. In him, I glimpse my own childhood echoes: the girl who, in grade five and later eight, stared blankly at test questions, ignoring teachers' whispered answers because they rang hollow without understanding. "You could've aced it," they'd chide upon returning my papers, but full marks meant nothing if the path to truth remained obscured. I'd pore over textbooks post-exam, piecing together the puzzle at my pace, realising the studied passage had morphed in the question's guise. To them, I was strange, doubting the authority who crafted the test. To me, it was integrity: accepting unearned knowledge felt like self-betrayal. Others labelled me "weird"; I saw righteousness in my quest for genuine insight.

And here lies the climax of our revelation: neurodivergence isn't a flaw to fix—it's a superior lens, a purer way of being that society, in its rush toward "normalcy," has tragically forgotten. These minds—unfettered by conformity—offer clarity we desperately need, reminding us that evolution thrives on diversity, not sameness. In reclaiming this truth, we honour not just Ilyas but ourselves, forging a world where every ability illuminates the path ahead

Upon learning to work on our individual selves with daily practices to muster the maturity of knowing and advocating for society's greater good, this journey will not end. Yet it is not a difficult journey if we empathise with people of determination and consider others around us in every step we take. This journey will prove to be fun once we realise the joy of sharing our experiences and not leaving others behind just because of a physical or mental impairment. Observe your world and find that your child might have a dyslexic classmate, your neighbour might be hard of hearing, your colleague might be visually impaired, or the weird cashier at the supermarket is autistic. Observe and sensitise and look for opportunities to help them feel involved, belonging in a community.

I remember being in a conversation with some ladies who were making fun of another, calling her strange because of some of her habits. One habit included her smiling to herself at the mirror every time she checked her hair was straight. I was the only one who defended her and asked, "Why does that make her weird?" Later I found out that the lady is in fact autistic (Asperger's disease). This goes to show how we are judgemental and insensitive, with gossip and conformist habits prevailing over empathy.

Conclusion

In the quiet aftermath of our shared journey through these pages, let us pause to distil the essence of what we've uncovered together. At its core, *Raising Me* offers these top five takeaways to guide your path forward: First, self-awareness is the cornerstone of transformation—by raising ourselves through practices like observing, sensing, and reflecting, we unlock deeper empathy for our children and others, turning personal growth into a ripple of change. Second, neurodivergence is not a deficit but a vibrant thread in humanity's tapestry; embracing it challenges the myth of "normal" and fosters inclusive families where every member's unique light shines. Third, parenting extends beyond the home—it's a societal act, where advocating for diverse abilities in schools, communities, and beyond builds resilient bonds that honour all. Fourth, trust your instincts as a caregiver; while experts provide tools, a mother's (or father's) organic wisdom—honed through lived experience and generational lore—often holds the key to navigating challenges like therapies or daily struggles. Finally, inclusion is an active choice: by suspending biases and designing environments centred on strengths, we create ecosystems where neurodivergent individuals thrive, enriching us all.

This book's mission remains steadfast: to awaken societies from the confines of "normalcy," forging building blocks for joyful families amid a fast-paced world that erodes our connections. Through my story as an Emirati mother raising Ilyas—my autistic son who taught me to see the world anew—we've explored how acknowledging our human traits allows us to truly behold one another, from the smallest child to the oldest soul. It's a call to reclaim those meaningful ties with families, neighbours, and strangers, starting with the self, so that neurodivergence becomes a celebrated gift rather than a hidden challenge.

As you close this chapter of our dialogue, I invite you to reach out—I'd be delighted to hear your reflections, questions, or stories of your own journey toward inclusion. Whether it's a query about practical strategies or a shared experience that resonates with Ilyas's path, connect with me through the details in the "About the Author" section; your voice adds to this collective tapestry, and together, we can weave even stronger threads.

Now, with these tools in hand—the practices, insights, and empathy you've gathered—step boldly into action. When you

CONCLUSION

set this book down, begin with one small, empowering move: observe a moment in your day with fresh eyes, perhaps with a child or colleague, and let it spark a ripple of kindness. You hold the power to raise yourself, uplift those around you, and reshape society—go forth and live it, for every act of inclusion starts with you.

Endnotes

i. Bearss, K., Burrell, T. L., Smith, T., McAdam, D. B., & Scahill, L. (2015). Effect of parent training vs parent education on behavioral problems in children with autism spectrum disorder: A randomized clinical trial. *JAMA, 313*(15), 1524-1533. https://doi.org/10.1001/jama.2015.3150

ii. Wijaya, I., & Wisesa, A. (2022). Motherhood as leadership in enabling high-performance organization by nurturing millennials in a patriarchal culture: A conceptual revisit. *International Journal of Management, Entrepreneurship, Social Science and Humanities, 5*(2), 1-16. https://doi.org/10.31098/ijmesh.v5i2.1013

iii. Sneed, L., & Samelson, D. (2022). Effectiveness of parent-led applied behavior analysis at improving outcomes for parents of autistic children. *Journal of Social, Behavioral,* and *Health Sciences, 16*(1), 160-177. https://doi.org/10.5590/JSBHS.2022.16.1.12

iv. Büyük, D. S., & Özmen, D. (2025). Effectiveness of a parent empowerment program for parents of children with autism: A randomized controlled trial. Child: *Care, Health and Development, 51*(5), e70148. https://doi.org/10.1111/cch.70148

v. Raymaakers, K. (2019, May 1). *Modern Family Index shows real motherhood penalty in American workplace.* Bright Horizons. https://investors.brighthorizons.com/news-releases/news-release-details/modern-family-index-shows-real-motherhood-penalty-american

Author Bio

Hanaa Alabri is an Emirati mother whose world transformed when her son, Ilyas, was diagnosed with autism at the tender age of two and a half. Born and raised in the vibrant heart of Abu Dhabi, Hanaa has always drawn strength from her cultural roots, channelling her experiences into a passionate advocacy for inclusive societies that embrace individuals with disabilities and hidden neurodivergences. Trained in Applied Behavioural Analysis, she has gained profound insights not only into her parenting journey but also into her own undiagnosed autistic traits, fostering a deeper empathy that infuses her life and work with purpose and resilience.

Professionally, Hanaa serves in Abu Dhabi's government sector, contributing to an organisation dedicated to expanding the city's educational landscape—a role that aligns seamlessly with her vision of unlocking humanity's potential. Holding a BA in Public Relations and an LLM in Sustainable Development Law, she has navigated diverse industries with grace and determination: from aviation, where she confronted the judgemental undercurrents of recruitment; to national defence, mastering the art of strategic preparation and quick thinking; healthcare, where she honed skills in clear communication and meticulous documentation; and now education, exploring pathways for collective growth. Guided by core values of honesty, love, humility, and courage, Hanaa remains steadfast in harmonising her personal goals with the UAE's national vision, striving to build collaborative communities through her talents in graphic design, storytelling, and events coordination.

Beyond her career, Hanaa's heart lies in nurturing the next generation. She hosts weekly children's classes for her son and friends in her community, creating spaces where every child—neurotypical or neurodivergent—can thrive in an atmosphere of understanding and joy. Through her writing, Hanaa invites readers into her emotional tapestry of motherhood, urging society to weave inclusivity into its very fabric, one compassionate thread at a time.

Glossary

Abu Ilyas: The father of Ilyas. In many Arabic nations, men are called by their eldest son "Abu [eldest son's name]," instead of their actual first name as a form of respect for their social status.

ASD: Autism Spectrum Disorder.

ADHD: Attention Deficit Hyperactivity Disorder.

ABA: Applied Behaviour Analysis. This type of therapy is often used for children with autism and other developmental disorders, focusing on improving skills such as social skills, communication, and learning.

BCBA: Board Certified Behavior Analyst. This is a graduate-level certification in behavioural analysis, granted by the Behavior Analyst Certification Board (BACB). BCBAs are trained professionals responsible for designing, implementing, and supervising behaviour intervention programs.

Dhikr: The devotional act of remembering and invoking Allah through repetitive recitation of His names, attributes, or other sacred phrases.

Diverse-abilities: Those who have different levels of abilities, covering delays in development.

Echolalia: Repetition of words just spoken by another person, occurring as a symptom of mental conditions.

Eid: An Islamic celebration. There are two for every Islamic year: Eid Al-Fitr at the end of Ramadan, and Eid Al Adha on the 11th day of Thoul Hijja, the pilgrimage month to celebrate those who completed their pilgrimage in Macca.

Hanoona: A nickname given to girls named Hana. In Arabic families, it is common to nickname children, such as Hamoodi for Mohamed, evoking affection and nurturing their playful souls in their formative years.

Hidden disabilities: Disabilities that are not physical or not obvious, such as deaf, mute, neurodivergent (ASD, ADHD, dyslexia, dysgraphia...).

GLOSSARY

Kandoora: A white dress worn by men of the United Arab Emirates and others in the Gulf countries of the Arabic Peninsula.

Khulu': A divorce process that is initiated by the wife and not the husband.

Learning Support Assistant (LSA): An educational professional who supports students who require additional help in classrooms. They work closely with teachers to provide tailored assistance to students facing challenges such as learning difficulties, disabilities, or language barriers. They are also known as Shadow Teachers.

Majlis: A formal living area in Emirati homes where guests are received. Usually every house has two majlis: one for men and another for women.

Nafas: The period of 40 days straight after giving birth when a mother is focused on healing and breastfeeding. Many women opt to do this at their mother's house, or their mothers stay with them.

OT: Occupational Therapy. This is a branch of healthcare that focuses on helping individuals perform everyday activities, particularly after changes in their physical or mental health. It involves customised interventions designed to assist people in overcoming physical, emotional, and social challenges, enabling them to safely participate in their daily routines.

POD: People of Determination—that is, people who have disabilities, whether physical, developmental or mental. Introduced in 2017, "People of Determination" was launched by His Highness Sheikh Mohammed bin Rashid Al Maktoum as part of a broader commitment to empower those with disabilities, replacing outdated labels with one that celebrates strength and potential.

QABA: Qualified Applied Behaviour Analysis Credentialing Board. This was established to meet the growing need for more credentialed professionals providing Applied Behavior Analysis (ABA) services. QABA certificants are trained in all aspects of ABA with qualification in autism and related disorders.

Quran: The holy book of Allah's words in Islam.

Shadow Teacher: Learning Support Assistant (see above).

ST: Speech Therapy, the assessment and treatment of communication problems and speech disorders. It is a specialised healthcare service provided by speech-language pathologists (SLPs), aimed at diagnosing and treating difficulties related to speech, language, voice, and social communication. The goal of speech therapy is to improve communication abilities, enabling individuals to engage meaningfully with their environment.

Student of Determination: A student who has a disability.

Ummah: Muslim nation or religious community.